Cambridge Elements

Elements in Philosophy of Law
edited by
George Pavlakos
University of Glasgow
Gerald J. Postema
University of North Carolina at Chapel Hill
Kenneth M. Ehrenberg
University of Surrey

Associate Editor
Sally Zhu
University of Sheffield

CONTEMPORARY NON-POSITIVISM

Emad H. Atiq
Cornell University

Shaftesbury Road, Cambridge CB2 8EA, United Kingdom

One Liberty Plaza, 20th Floor, New York, NY 10006, USA

477 Williamstown Road, Port Melbourne, VIC 3207, Australia

314–321, 3rd Floor, Plot 3, Splendor Forum, Jasola District Centre,
New Delhi – 110025, India

103 Penang Road, #05–06/07, Visioncrest Commercial, Singapore 238467

Cambridge University Press is part of Cambridge University Press & Assessment,
a department of the University of Cambridge.

We share the University's mission to contribute to society through the pursuit of
education, learning and research at the highest international levels of excellence.

www.cambridge.org
Information on this title: www.cambridge.org/9781009539128

DOI: 10.1017/9781009288293

© Emad H. Atiq 2025

This publication is in copyright. Subject to statutory exception and to the provisions
of relevant collective licensing agreements, no reproduction of any part may take
place without the written permission of Cambridge University Press & Assessment.

When citing this work, please include a reference to the DOI 10.1017/9781009288293

First published 2025

A catalogue record for this publication is available from the British Library

ISBN 978-1-009-53912-8 Hardback
ISBN 978-1-009-28830-9 Paperback
ISSN 2631-5815 (online)
ISSN 2631-5807 (print)

Cambridge University Press & Assessment has no responsibility for the persistence
or accuracy of URLs for external or third-party internet websites referred to in this
publication and does not guarantee that any content on such websites is, or will
remain, accurate or appropriate.

Contemporary Non-Positivism

Elements in Philosophy of Law

DOI: 10.1017/9781009288293
First published online: February 2025

Emad H. Atiq
Cornell University

Author for correspondence: Emad H. Atiq, eha47@cornell.edu

Abstract: This Element defends and clarifies the thesis that the legality of a system of rules depends on its moral features. Positivists who deny this dependence struggle to explain: (1) the traditional classification of moral norms as a form of a priori law; (2) judicial reliance on moral norms in legal discovery; (3) persistent theoretical disagreement about intra-systemic, law-determining facts; (4) why radically arbitrary or immoral schemes of social organization represent borderline cases of law; and (5) why law, like other artifacts, can be evaluated in a kind-relative sense ("as law"). Meanwhile, traditional versions of non-positivism overstate the dependence going further than the desiderata warrant. A moderate theory is formulated: law is an artifact whose existence depends on adequately performing an essentially normative function. The theory's justification lies in its explanatory power: a comparison with other "value-driven" artifacts, such as artworks, proves vital for understanding legal language, reasoning, and practice.

Keywords: legal rules, moral principles, concepts of law, goodness-fixing kinds, normative artifacts

© Emad H. Atiq 2025

ISBNs: 9781009539128 (HB), 9781009288309 (PB), 9781009288293 (OC)
ISSNs: 2631-5815 (online), 2631-5807 (print)

Contents

1 Introduction: Subject Matter and Methodology   1

2 The Argument Against Positivism   10

3 How to Be a Legal Non-Positivist   35

4 Outstanding Questions   68

References   73

1 Introduction: Subject Matter and Methodology

Legal systems exhibit certain necessary or otherwise systematic features. For instance, it is hard to imagine a legal system without rules that prescribe or prohibit forms of behavior. Legal systems seem also to involve power relations and the use of a characteristic language of obligations, entitlements, and responsibilities. Philosophers of law are interested in identifying such features, their degree of generalizability, and, ultimately, whether the general features are amenable to philosophical explanation – that is, an explanation in terms of the nature or grounds of law. And one prominent view, or family of views, maintains that law necessarily exhibits certain *normative* features that bear on what law, essentially, is. On this way of thinking, in order for a scheme of social organization to constitute a legal system, it must satisfy not just non-normative criteria, such as having prescriptive or proscriptive rules, but essentially normative criteria as well, such as being to some extent good, or rational, or just.

The view is known in the literature as "legal non-positivism" or "anti-positivism," which is an unfortunate name for several reasons. Besides being drab and not very informative, it implies that what unifies the research program is the rejection of some other view – namely, positivism. Positivists emphasize social facts and social criteria to the exclusion of the normative in their account of whether and why a society counts as having a legal system – roughly, facts concerning what members of the society believe, say, do, or desire. However, not all views inconsistent with positivism are conventionally discussed under the rubric of "non-positivism," nor are they all covered by this text, which focuses on several contemporary strands. If anything, it is the aforementioned normative thesis about law that, once suitably clarified, happens to be universally rejected by positivists and that serves as our unifying principle.

Some justification for conventional labels may be found in the fact that legal positivism serves as an excellent starting point for philosophical discussions about law. Not because positivism is the default or leading view of law's nature (a claim positivists sometimes make but that finds little support in actual empirical studies investigating the views of contemporary philosophers, jurists, and the folk) or because it came first in the history of legal philosophy (it didn't). Legal positivism serves as our point of departure for intellectual reasons – that is, for its simplicity as a general theory of law, parsimony, and ability to explain much of what needs explaining about law without recourse to the kinds of controversial assumptions that non-positivists typically help themselves to. Since we want our theory of law to exhibit virtues like simplicity (even as non-positivists), it is best to see how far we can satisfy our descriptive and explanatory ambitions based on positivist assumptions alone. On this telling, positivism as a characterization of law in the juridical sense bears the same relation to its subject matter as Newtonian physics does to the physical laws – of being a powerful approximation, adequate for most practical purposes, but perhaps less than fully accurate.

HLA Hart's (1960) view, the most influential of all positivist accounts, is helpfully illustrative of the assumptions and explanatory focus of positivists. Hart was impressed by, among other things, the form or structure of legal systems. Legal systems paradigmatically, and perhaps universally, exhibit a certain hierarchical form. They consist of rules that prescribe or prohibit forms of conduct, but there are also rules for determining, changing, and figuring out the rules of the system. Hart was impressed, also, by the fact that participants in legal systems seem to employ a "characteristic ... normative terminology" of what people *ought* to do or are *permitted* to do, and, moreover, that they seem to follow the laws in a way that cannot be characterized as unreflective obedience (p. 56). Rather, participants within legal systems – especially those who enjoy an "official" status within the system – present the law *as worth following*. Such reflections led Hart to the view that legal systems are, essentially, a kind of social order that (1) exhibits a hierarchical structure consisting of first-order rules as well as higher-order rules – so-called "rules of recognition, change, and adjudication"; and (2) includes fundamental rules that are followed by members of a community based on certain normative assumptions that together comprise what Hart called the "internal point of view" on the rules.

What makes Hart's theory a positivistic account of law isn't his emphasis on the formal structure of legal systems or on the attitudes held by officials and others in such systems (normative or otherwise); it's a further claim of the form: "... and that's it." Hart's view is positivistic because any social order, no matter how vicious, irrational, or bizarre (with some important caveats that we'll get to), counts as a legal system, so long as it manifests the relevant structure and certain social facts regarding people's attitudes towards the rules obtain. Other positivists have emphasized other putatively necessary features of law, such as the existence of power relations, especially, power relations between a sovereign and subordinates, or the use of sanctions to elicit obedience (Austin 1832 [1995]). But all agree that social, and perhaps structural, facts alone can account for law's existence. More recently, positivists have tended to acknowledge certain qualified connections between law and normativity – for example, that law necessarily deals with matters of moral concern, makes moral claims, and entails certain morally evaluable risks (Raz 1994; Shapiro 2011: p. 212; Green & Adams 2019; cf. Hart 1958: p. 619). But no positivist worthy of the name has ever conceded that a social order's legality necessarily depends on its merits, in a robustly normative sense of "merit" (Gardner 2001).

While positivist accounts of law such as Hart's have shed considerable light on the nature of legal systems and legal objectivity, they are vulnerable to challenge. For legal orders exhibit a broad range of features that aren't so easily explained if positivism is true, some of which it takes a degree of immersion in legal history and practice to appreciate. Section 2 catalogs these features, which concern: the role of moral and more broadly normative considerations in legal reasoning, both historically (2.1) and in contemporary legal practice (2.2); the nature and persistence of intra-systemic legal disagreement (2.3); the intuitive distinction between bona fide legal systems and social orders established by powerful organizations devoted to the criminal and the absurd (2.4); and the fact that the law lends itself to both functional and kind-relative normative appraisal (2.5). Overall, this section develops and consolidates the argument against positivism drawing on recent scholarship not just in philosophy but in legal history and social psychology as well. Section 3 explores the different forms of non-positivism in the literature that have been motivated based on positivism's explanatory gaps, including natural law theory (Section 3.1), Dworkinian interpretivism and the "one-system view" (Section 3.2), as well as dual character and aggregative cluster accounts of the concept of law (Section 3.3). After highlighting some problems for these more traditional views, I argue for a moderate form of non-positivism that forges several surprising connections across theories (Section 3.4). The main upshot is that we cannot make sense of legal systems and their characteristic features without recourse to some genuinely normative criteria and without an account of the metaphysics of normativity. But, as I explain in Section 4, questions concerning the content of the relevant norms and the nature of normativity remain unsettled in ways that define an agenda for future work.

Let me note at the outset that the discussion is centered on ideas and arguments, rather than persons and personalities, an approach I take to be essential for moving the debate forward. This text does not aspire to be a comprehensive summary or review of every contribution to legal philosophy made by its major or prominent figures. There are plenty of excellent resources on the history of jurisprudence that do just that. Instead, my goal is to foreground what I take to be the most important issues, the most interesting arguments, and the most compelling observations on which an original and attractive set of answers to the traditional questions of jurisprudence can be based. That said, by the end of the discussion, we will have covered more than enough ground to enable the engaged reader to contribute intelligently to the full spectrum of philosophical debates about the nature of law.

In preparation for the more substantive discussions to follow, the remainder of this introductory section makes a few more observations about methodology.

Hopefully, the way I've described the project of legal philosophy sets it apart from others with which it is often conflated, such as projects within lexical semantics or practical ethics. As I see it, the central project of legal philosophy is descriptive, explanatory, and synthetic: the goal is to catalog what legal rules and practices are generally like and to develop a theory of law that explains the systematic features while being consistent with our considered views on related matters, such as the nature of rules, group agency, language, and morality. Since not everyone shares this vision of legal philosophy, the remainder of this section is devoted to correcting some common misconceptions about the subject, several of which are surprisingly common even among philosophers. Those who feel confident in their sense of the methodology should feel free to skip ahead to Section 2 or, alternatively, return to Section 1 once they have seen the methodology in action.

1.1 Analytic Jurisprudence and Conceptual Analysis

As I've suggested, the starting point for legal philosophy is some candidate feature of law or legal systems that is putatively necessary or, at the very least, systematic in a way that invites explanation. Where, one wonders, does evidence of a feature's necessity come from? Philosophers rely on ordinary observations about *actual* legal systems, of course. But they also rely on conceptual intuition, especially when exploring the space of all possible systems of law.[1] For instance, it seems like a conceptual truth that wherever there is law, there are systems of more-or-less explicit rules and, plausibly, rules that attract some form of social acceptance. Moreover, as we'll discover shortly, philosophers often motivate their accounts of law based on meta-semantic intuitions, such as intuitions about when and why parties who disagree about the content of the law are disagreeing about a common subject matter (and not just talking past each other).

All of this fosters the impression that legal philosophy is fundamentally interested in language – in particular, the concept or application criteria associated with the ordinary term "law" – perhaps with the ultimate goal of supplanting the not-very-informative definitions currently in the dictionary. Motivated by this vision of philosophy's aims, some contemporary philosophers have adopted the experimental methods of social psychology to test how subjects who are trained in neither law nor philosophy use legal terminology in response to philosophical thought experiments (Donelson & Hannikainen 2020; Flanagan & Hannikainen 2020; Tobia 2022).

---

[1] Raz's (2002: p. 159) reflections on the possibility of law in a society of angels powerfully illustrates this method.

Our setup of the problem should help clarify why legal philosophy is not exclusively or even primarily concerned with ordinary language or meaning. Philosophers writing in this area certainly *use* the concept of law to help fix a target of analysis (Raz 1979: p. 221). By the concept of law, I mean the broadly shared application criteria or usage rules associated with a term in ordinary language: "law" as employed in juridical contexts.[2] We deploy our own understanding of this concept when we decide whether this or that actual or imaginary social order constitutes a legal system. And more generally, much of philosophy consists in scrutinizing the concepts we use and even revising our overall conceptual framework to keep it in order, since we often don't know which of our concepts (including meta-concepts) need refining until their deficiencies become salient to us through systematic reflection. So, philosophers can be said to both use ordinary concepts and deploy a kind of conceptual expertise, one that's earned through careful reflection on a broad range of relatively basic and important concepts.

But ultimately, ordinary terms and the shared concepts they express serve as mere steppingstones, useful for the purpose of drawing attention to a phenomenon that is interesting in its own right, and that may or may not be, in the present context, the exclusive referent or meaning of the term "law." The phenomenon of interest is a *kind* or *category* of normative system that is reflected in our general reasoning about social orders and their objective features – a form of reasoning that philosophical thought experiments and arguments more broadly are designed to elicit.[3] By analogy, the term "water" is ordinarily used to pick out different things in different contexts – often (though by no means always) the potable stuff in rivers, lakes, and streams with its standard percentages of isotopic isomers; but in other, more scientific contexts, a specific substance with a particular constitution. Scientists are no more beholden to ordinary usage, contexts, and meaning than philosophers of law, and appreciating this fact does not require an extended detour through the philosophy of vernacular kind terms (see, e.g., Putnam 1973; Kripke 1980). The category reflected in philosophically informed reasoning about laws and legal systems may not be *semantically* magnetic, in the sense of being a fitting candidate for the shared meaning of a publicly available term. But it might still be worth elucidating if it happens to be implicit in our considered

---

[2] The points to follow do not turn on any particular theory of concepts, criterial or otherwise. The observations hold just as well on inferentialist and use-theoretic accounts of the nature of concepts. See, e.g., Dummett (1993), Brandom (1994).

[3] For related points, see Marmor (2013) and Finnis (2007: p. 276): "There is no point in trying to explain a common-sense concept which takes its meanings from its very varied contexts ... My purpose has not been to explain an unfocused 'ordinary concept' but to develop a concept for use in a theoretical explanation."

reflections about an objective aspect of the world – that is, if it is *cognitively magnetic*.[4]

That said, how closely legal philosophers hew to what participants in legal practice are tracking using legal terminology may determine how much interest there is outside philosophy in its subject matter. I'll point out later that legal positivists may have retreated to an overly provincial subject by neglecting to consider how legal experts within legal systems reason about law. But for now, we should stay alive to the possibility that the topic of interest – roughly, the nature of a kind that corresponds to, among other things, certain distinctions we are disposed to draw upon reflection between normative systems – may be interesting in its own right, regardless of whether it corresponds perfectly to the ordinary concept of law. At the same time, no philosophical account of the nature of a kind could be complete that didn't include some understanding of the linguistic expressions we use to refer to it. In the same vein, no one thinks that a complete metaphysics of morality could afford to ignore the nature and function of moral language. To sum up the point of this subsection, we shouldn't dismiss (informed) conceptual intuitions about law as irrelevant to the philosophy of law nor take the examination of a concept in shared use as its final goal.[5]

1.2 The Metaphysical Turn in Contemporary Jurisprudence

For the reasons discussed, the present task is to develop a satisfying account of the nature of a kind of social order, an account that explains the regular features of its instances. We can call the property that instances of the kind share "the property of being a legal system" so long as we bear in mind the caveats about tying the subject matter of jurisprudence too closely to a shared concept or ordinary term. In the terminology of contemporary metaphysics, we're interested in the essence and grounds of *being a legal system* – or what it is in virtue of that a set of rules get to be *legal* (cf. Rosen 2010; Marmor 2013; Chilovi & Pavlakos 2019; but see Tripkovic & Patterson 2023). One hopes that an account of the grounds of legality construed as a property of a *system* of rules will shed light, also, on the grounds of the legality of specific *rules* within any such

---

[4] A category is cognitively magnetic in the stipulative sense I intend here if its fittingness for use in cognition becomes apparent through ideal reflection. A category might be relevantly useful because it carves nature at its joints (leaning, here, on the more familiar concept of semantic magnetism developed by Lewis (1984)) or for other reasons, such as convenience and fit with a broader conceptual scheme.

[5] How much does the methodology I'm recommending here differ from the view of "conceptual analysis" offered by Jackson (1998: pp. 42–44) and Chalmers & Jackson (2001)? In a nutshell, their approach seems overly constrained by ordinary conceptual intuitions; it isn't clear how much room there is on their view for revising the categories we use based on theoretical considerations of consistency, explanatory adequacy, simplicity, and fit with a larger conceptual scheme. But a serious discussion of this issue would take us too far afield.

system – or what legal philosophers sometimes call "the criteria of legal validity."[6]

Let me say briefly why this approach to setting up the issues does not involve any dubious metaphysical assumptions. Talk of kinds, kind-properties, and their essences might seem controversial in the context of understanding the social world. As a colleague once put it to me, "unlike water, law is not a 'thing' out in the world whose 'nature' can be investigated under a microscope." It's true, of course, that we cannot point at the property that philosophers of law are interested in – the property of *being a legal system* – the same way we can point to water to make it the shared subject matter of investigation. But that's true of specific *laws* as well, construed as rules or norms, whose existence and amenability to investigation we have no reason to doubt. And the fact that properties and other abstracta have essential natures can be motivated using ordinary examples. We know that the property *being red* essentially involves *being a color*. *Being an animal* essentially involves *being concrete*. *Being a triangle* essentially involves *being trilateral and triangular*. Whether some properties are similarly essential to *being law* or *being a legal system* is a perfectly coherent question, even if the answer is not straightforward.[7]

Still, there are at least two kinds of concerns one might have about the framework that I'll note here, but for reasons of space won't be able to address fully. The first relates to the abstract as such. Some philosophers deny the existence of properties and, indeed, *all* abstracta – namely, nominalists (see, e.g., Goodman & Quine 1947). But their doubts about the abstract are perfectly general. Since talk of properties comes naturally to legal philosophers – indeed, it seems to be common ground in legal philosophy that there *are* abstract entities – we can set such general doubts aside.

The second concern is more pressing and has to do with the possibility of a shared subject matter. What ensures that within the philosophy of law (setting aside more general discourses about law), theorists are all investigating the same thing, the same kind or property? What secures a common subject matter in the philosophy of law is agreement in our observations about the regular

---

[6] The precise relationship between the legality of a system of rules and the legality of specific rules within a system is explored in subsequent sections.

[7] On the essential properties of abstracta, see Fine (1994) and Zalta (2006). Roughly, the essential properties of an abstract object are included in our conception of the object. To borrow one of Zalta's examples, *being a detective* is essential to *being Sherlock Holmes*, given that our conception of the fictional character plausibly "encodes" his being a detective. The fact that our conception of an object encodes some property needn't be transparent to reflection. Some conceptual commitments are "discovered" because they are nonobviously entailed by other, more transparent commitments. Many technical concepts that have worked their way into public consciousness are used without complete mastery of their nature (see, e.g., Burge 1979). I think this is true of legal concepts.

features of law that call out for explanation – that is, agreement about the desiderata that constrain a philosophical account of legality. But the concern is a perfectly legitimate one because philosophers often *don't* share all the same assumptions about law's necessary or explanatorily relevant features. So, we should stay alive to the possibility that positivists and non-positivists might be categorizing social orders differently, and analyzing distinct categories as a result, in ways that are on a par in terms of their ability to track objective features of and distinctions within the social domain. But we cannot know whether that's true without engaging with the dialectic. Even if it turns out that the philosophy of law has given us two coherent means of categorizing social orders, the fact that exchange between these two camps persists and has persisted for as long as it has suggests that there is enough overlap in their reasoning about law for exchange to be productive – that is, for both positivist and non-positivist philosophers to learn from each other about which regular features of law invite explanation and how the explanatory puzzles might be resolved.

1.3 Conceptual Engineering and Practical Philosophy

Since a fully general account of the nature of legality may have implications about the content of the law in particular jurisdictions, and since what the law is, "here" or elsewhere, is often a high-stakes matter, the philosophy of law is vulnerable to a kind of pragmatic encroachment. That is, pragmatic considerations may influence theory choice, with participants in philosophical debate embracing some view in the hopes that its wide acceptance, including by legal officials, will lead to positive outcomes in society.[8] This might happen implicitly, as when we engage in motivated reasoning. Or it can happen openly when the explicit aim of inquiry is to "engineer" a concept or category, call it LAW*, that, if widely embraced, is likely to promote outcomes we care about, regardless of whether it is consistent with our intuitive or ordinary ways of categorizing social orders (see, e.g., Waldron 2001; Murphy 2008; Jiménez 2023).

In fact, a growing body of literature suggests that debates about the nature of law, along with other debates in philosophy, are disguised "meta-linguistic negotiations" (Plunkett & Sundell 2013a; Plunkett 2016). A meta-linguistic negotiation occurs when parties who seemingly disagree about the nature of some subject are implicitly negotiating how the referring term should be used going forward while using the term as though their preferred semantic rules were already in place. Participants in meta-linguistic negotiations may be indifferent to what the term *actually* refers to and the correct semantic rules

---

[8] On the practical and ideological uses to which jurisprudence is sometimes put, see Atiq and Mathews (2022).

implicit in general usage. But pretending that their own use of the term conforms to existing rules is an essential aspect of their persuasive strategy.

There are still more nuanced accounts of the role of pragmatic considerations in the philosophy of law. Joseph Raz (1979), for example, argues explicitly that philosophical analyses of categories like law may be driven in large part by the need to explain certain settled features of law, but that there is room for practical considerations, along with considerations of clarity and consistency with a broader conceptual scheme, to refine our conception of law, and even to modify it insofar as its precise contours are underdetermined. But none of these views offer quite the same vision of legal philosophy as the one outlined above. While I share Plunkett and Sundell's view that philosophers don't necessarily use ordinary terms in ordinary ways (indeed, philosophical arguments such as intuition pumps are often designed to put pressure on ordinary concepts), I reject at least two claims that are either entailed or strongly implied by their proposed interpretation: (1) that it doesn't matter to participants in these debates whether they are using a shared term to express a shared concept, and (2) that the considerations that motivate participants are primarily pragmatic.[9] The meta-linguistic negotiation account in its most unqualified form seems to me flawed, since it flies in the face of serious reflection on the nature of philosophical disagreement by participants in these debates and, also, since metalinguistic negotiation seems to me to be both morally and rationally objectionable in philosophical and legal exchange, even if it might be a more acceptable communicative strategy in more playful contexts.

In any case, this text's central task is emphatically *not* to lay out a practical case for non-positivism (or a practical case for how we should use the term "law" going forward). I shall defend non-positivism, simply, as an accurate characterization of a kind, *law*, that regulates our considered judgments about the general and necessary features of legal rules, a defense that should be evaluated on those terms. Although non-positivists have sometimes relied on pragmatic considerations to defend their account, I will not be summarizing such arguments because, even if we assume their relevance, I am simply not sure which way the pragmatic considerations cut. Whether judges and other legal officials would behave better if they were to embrace a non-positivistic

---

[9] See, e.g., Plunkett and Sundell's (2013a: pp. 14–17) discussion of disagreements over the spiciness of a meal or the criteria for being an athlete. On their interpretation of bedrock juridical disagreements, jurists with different concepts of law "negotiate how words should be used" and "pragmatically advocate" for their preferred concept (2013b: pp. 242, 264–267). In fact, the application of their theory to disagreements in which participants explicitly contest the metalinguistic characterization is far from straightforward. See discussion in Rudolph (2023). For an alternative account of legal disagreements that doesn't necessarily involve ascribing different concepts of law to judges (or philosophers) with superficially incompatible conceptions, see 3.4.

conception of law seems to me to be a hard question for moral philosophy and social science. It isn't a question for the descriptive metaphysician. And so, the focus in what follows is on observations about legality that, as far as I can tell, are non-normative and *a*political, cry out for explanation, and aren't so easily explained by a positivistic conception of law.

2 The Argument Against Positivism

The order in which I review the considerations to follow does not track the order in which they were introduced into legal philosophy. It is an order that seems most logical to me and reflects my convictions about how the overall case against positivism ought to be structured to be maximally compelling. For instance, some readers might expect the section to lead with Ronald Dworkin's influential observations about moral principles and theoretical disagreement in law. But I hope to persuade such readers that postponing our engagement with Dworkin until after we've surveyed the historical facts in 2.1 helps us see the force of his arguments more clearly. At the same time, I've endeavored to distinguish the considerations on which a case against positivism might be built from the "camp" with which they are associated. The arguments we're about to discuss appeal not just to considerations raised by non-positivists but also to observations made by positivists whose implications have yet to be fully drawn out. Arguments that favor specific versions of non-positivism, rather than non-positivism generally, are addressed in Section 3. The focus for now is on considerations of general significance.

2.1 Moral Principles in Legal History

A remarkably regular feature of legal systems across recorded history, including the legal systems of ancient Egypt, Greece, Rome, early modern Europe, and pre-twentieth-century America, concerns the account offered by legal officials of the content of the law, an account included in primary legal texts. The law, it was said, included certain principles of rationality and justice whose legality was supposed to be self-evident.[10] Such claims did not go uncontested; both the content of this alleged body of a priori law and its very possibility were routinely disputed. But a commitment to at least some such laws was sufficiently standard to be taught to new students of law in universities.[11] For instance, a principle of impartiality, forbidding any person from being a judge

---

[10] The historical literature on the subject is rich. For a survey and its significance for legal philosophy, see Atiq (2023).

[11] To pick just a few illustrative studies, see Helmholz (2015), Grey (1978), Corwin (1928), Pollock (1902), and Vander Waerdt (1994).

in their own cause (*nemo iudex in causa sua*), has been presented at various times as a paradigmatic example of a priori law.[12] A principle of reciprocity, imposing reciprocal duties on sovereign and subject, enjoyed a similar status in early English common law: of being law that applies *ex proprio vigore*.[13] Legal officials, including individuals tasked with law-discovery, believed that they could rely on such principles to resolve disputes and obligate both subjects and sovereign regardless of the existence of local statutes, legitimating customs, agreements, or constitutions. The Romans called it "natural law," but the principles were given many other names at different times and in different systems, including "moral law," "unchangeable law," and even the "the law of laws."[14] During the early modern period, especially, legal texts explicitly distinguished these principles as a form of "natural," universally applicable, and default law from what they called "positive law," or law *posited* by states and persons.

Three key features of this practice are worth emphasizing: (1) the fact that jurists classified principles of rationality and morality as "law" (or "lex" or "jus"), (2) that they deemed the legality of the principles a priori, and (3) the fact that the principles of a priori legality were consequential within the system in light of the broader practice of legal officials and other actors. To elaborate on this third point, the principles of a priori law were employed by judges and lawyers in thoroughly practical ways, including to resolve disputes, constrain kings, queens, and legislatures, and fill gaps in other posited law, such as statutory or precedential law. These contextual facts suggest that the relevant judgments of law track the juridical sense of interest, and not the many other senses of "law" that find expression in such phrases as "the laws of mathematics" or "the law of thermodynamics." Later, we shall discuss a philosophical position that the literature dubs "natural law theory" and its relationship to this practice. But our present observations concern an entirely ordinary (i.e., non-philosophical) regularity: a practice visible in both civil and common law traditions, at least until the turn of the twentieth century.[15]

What is a legal positivist to make of this history?[16] Neither the classification of a principle like *nemo iudex in causa sua* as a form of law nor the explanations

---

[12] See Yale (1974). For illustrative cases, see City of London v Wood (1702), 88 ER 1592 at 1602, Thomas Bonham v College of Physicians (1610), 77 ER 646 at 652.

[13] See discussion in Price (1997). As Price points out, "natural law or unwritten, fundamental law – law that was beyond the reach of the customary or municipal law" – was the basis for the holding in the famous case of *Calvin v. Smith* 1608, 77 ER 377 at 392, establishing birthright citizenship in England for Scottish-born subjects after King James I became King of England (p. 96). The case itself and the context in which it was decided are well worth examining for understanding the salience and supremacy of the "law of reason" in early English common law.

[14] See sources cited and discussion in Atiq (2023: p. 52).   [15] See sources cited Note 11.

[16] Hart discusses the history of the principles of legality only in passing. See discussion in Waldron (2008a).

jurists gave for *why* the principle counts as self-evident and universal law seem consistent with positivism. Positivists maintain that a principle's legality cannot obtain independently of jurisdiction-specific social facts, such as facts about local customs or rules of recognition. But that seems to have been explicitly denied by ordinary legal officials, as part of their official story about the content of their law. The a priori laws were not "derived" from more fundamental legal rules. Their legal force was portrayed as independent of jurisdiction-specific customs or conventions. And in several of these systems, jurists did not all agree about the appropriateness of relying on the principles of "natural law." And yet a significant and visible number of jurists nevertheless did.[17] Given this background, the positivist's explanatory options appear limited (for a more detailed analysis, see Atiq 2023).

One option would be to dismiss the historical claims as myths borne of a premodern conception of the world. Past jurists were simply mistaken in their assessment of either the content of the law or the reasons for legality. But the mistake should seem puzzling if we assume positivism's truth. Of course, people have been mistaken about all sorts of things over the course of human history. Far too often they have been mistaken about what justice requires. But it is unclear why past jurists would have been so mistaken about the grounds of legality, especially if we assume that positivists are right that the grounds are purely social. For if we assume positivism, then there appears to be no connection between the grounds of law and jurists' apparently mistaken beliefs about it, which is odd because regular and systematic mistakes about a *category* in ordinary use aren't usually disconnected in this way from its nature. Bear in mind that officials treated the legality of the principles of rationality and fairness as a priori or self-evident; it wasn't inferred based on complex arguments or considerations. Accordingly, positivists need to explain why officials embedded in these legal systems would be so mistaken about the concepts and categories they used. Whereas some systematic mistakes about law may well be explainable in terms of positivist assumptions,[18] the precise mistake that invites

---

[17] See Atiq (2023: pp. 48–49) for examples of explicit contestation.

[18] To illustrate, if we assume the truth of positivism, then perhaps it's no surprise that people have historically thought (falsely we may assume) that the gods or the spirits of the ancestors determine law. According to positivism, social facts ground law, which can, in principle, include facts involving the actions or desires of supernatural beings, especially beings with incredible power (recall Austinian positivism's emphasis on the power to coerce and command obedience). On this picture, our historical counterparts weren't confused about the a priori criteria of legality (which would be puzzling); they were confused about the social facts – specifically, facts about the kinds of beings that exist and their psychologies. One might be tempted to think that the positivist can tell a similar story about people's beliefs about moral principles. Since pre-modern societies are more likely to believe that the gods demand compliance with moral principles, they are more likely to treat these principles as *law*, even universal law given the gods' universal

explanation, here, is the tendency to see the *morality* or *rationality* of a principle as a sufficient (and self-evident) ground of its legality. And the need for an explanation is especially pressing given that, as we shall see in Section 3, more charitable interpretations of historical practice are possible that don't rely on any dubious premodern commitments.

An error theory that posits an unexplained gap between people's beliefs about when a concept applies a priori, on the one hand, and the truth about its application does not seem all that appealing. Alternatively, positivists might regard the concepts and categories employed within prior legal systems as simply distinct from the modern category of law (Watson 2022b). On this approach, most legal systems through the ages have relied on some other category, call it LAW*, that differs from the category of interest to contemporary philosophers. We might use similar or even identical terminology as our historical counterparts, but the sense or meaning of terms like "law," and, relatedly, our ways of categorizing social orders and normative systems, has changed over time. This approach has several virtues: (1) it refrains from positing widespread and unexplained errors within historical legal practice; (2) it is consistent with and, indeed, explains the fact that a commitment to "natural" or a priori law isn't nearly as widespread as it once was; and (c) the approach is consistent, also, with our methodological assumptions – in particular, the fact that philosophers aren't necessarily interested in ordinary concepts.

Nevertheless, the effort to carve out historical assumptions as irrelevant to the philosophical enterprise is theoretically costly for several reasons. One reason is that positivists have presented themselves as engaged in a debate about the nature of law not just with contemporary philosophers of law but with past thinkers, such as Aristotle, Pufendorf, Grotius, Aquinas, Austin, and others, who developed general theories of law at a time when the existence of "natural law" was widely embraced. And other than Austin, these philosophers were all committed to natural or a priori law, and were no doubt influenced by historical legal practice. Put differently, the philosophy of law isn't supposed to be

---

jurisdiction and authority. On this error theory, past jurists were implicitly applying social criteria in treating moral principles as law, albeit on the basis of false assumptions about the social facts. This effort to explain the phenomenon has the virtue of at least trying to forge a connection between people's mistakes about a category and its true nature. The problem, however, is that this just-so story ignores the fact that past legal cultures knew how to distinguish the "laws of god" from the "laws of reason," and routinely did (Atiq 2022: p. 45). It ignores, also, the fact that the legality of the principles of reason and justice was treated as *self-evident*, including within cultures that didn't think the gods were necessarily just or rational. By contrast, there were regular attempts to explain the legality of the commands of the gods in more basic terms, like their apparent authority over created beings. Thanks to Andrei Marmor for discussion on this point.

a response to some uniquely modern way of thinking about and categorizing normative systems or social orders.[19] It is supposed to deliver an account of a category in very broad and general use. So, thinking that there is some sharp divide between the juridical categories employed at different times entails conceding that at least some assumptions positivists make about law are deeply suspect. At the very least, avoiding legal history diminishes the significance of the positivist project, for it implies that the category under analysis is historically contingent and optional, at least in the absence of an explanation of why the historical category of LAW* is defective or no longer worth using.

A second problem with the appeal to conceptual change is that it doesn't *seem* like past cultures were operating with a distinct concept of law. The functional role of what they called "law" seems identical to that of our laws: laws are invoked to resolve disputes, constrain sovereign and subjects alike, and are cited in legal texts. This appearance is related to a point we'll discuss later, concerning the nature and persistence of legal disagreement among agents who differ dramatically in their views on the grounds of law. For now, note that the relative lack of explicit references to a category of self-evident natural law in contemporary legal practice needn't be evidence of conceptual change. After all, modern legal systems have absorbed many principles that were once introduced as self-evident laws of rationality and justice into their customary, precedential, and written constitutional laws. That is, the legality of the relevant principles may be overdetermined in modern legal systems, given their embeddedness in more familiar positive sources of law. Moreover, contemporary legal systems didn't appear ex nihilo. Many such systems present their laws and legal practices as inherited and to some extent continuous with the past (Postema 2019; Priel 2020). To draw on an example from the legal system I'm most familiar with, American constitutional lawyers routinely defer to historical understandings of legal terminology. At the very least, they view past practices as a constraint on contemporary interpretations of the law. Given such diachronic deference dispositions, it remains an unsettled question whether and to what extent contemporary legal practice is informed by historical assumptions about the status of moral principles. Certainly, when viewed in the light of legal history, certain aspects of modern legal systems become harder for positivists to explain, an issue we turn to next.

---

[19] Both Hart (1994: p. 240) and Raz (2004: p. 348) suggest, albeit in passing, that their explanatory focus is on the features of a modern legal system. But they fail to engage with the question of whether our modern conception of a legal system differs from or is continuous with the historical conception. Moreover, they present themselves as disagreeing with their historical counterparts on the nature of law. See Postema (2018) on why we should be skeptical of efforts to limit the temporal scope of philosophical inquiry.

2.2 Moral Principles in Adjudication

One of Ronald Dworkin's (1967, 1974, 1986) most important observations about contemporary legal practice concerned the way judges engage in moral and evaluative reasoning to resolve legal disputes. Judges are responsible for figuring out the law as it bears on a dispute, and in discharging this responsibility, frequently base their legal conclusions on considerations of justice and fairness. Dworkin (1967) offered two principal illustrations in his classic: *Model of Rules I*. *Henningsen v Bloomfield Motors Inc.* involved a contracts dispute concerning the interpretation and enforceability of a warranty provision that purported to limit the defendant's exposure to liability.[20] In refusing to enforce the defendant's interpretation of the provision, the court observed that "courts generally refuse to lend themselves to the enforcement of a 'bargain' in which one party has unjustly taken advantage of the economic necessities of the other."[21] On Dworkin's portrayal, the judge was guided by considerations of justice in reaching a *legal* conclusion: the unenforceability of the contractual provision. Dworkin's other example was *Riggs v Palmer* (p. 29).[22] The legal question in that case was whether the defendant's will should be invalidated to prevent a named beneficiary from inheriting who had been involved in the defendant's murder. The court found that no statute under either probate or criminal law and no prior judicial decision invalidated the will. Nevertheless, the court refused to enforce it, appealing to what it termed "universal law": the principle that "no one shall be permitted to profit by his own fraud, or to take advantage of his own wrong."[23]

It is easy to multiply examples of similar cases involving judges invoking morality in the interpretation and application of legal rules. Moral principles have a role to play not just in the law of contracts and estates, but in virtually every domain of law, especially when laws are crafted using ostensibly moral concepts, such as, for example, in tort law (the common law of negligence forbids "unreasonable" risk-taking), criminal law (a sentencing statute might restrict the maximum penalty to "heinous" crimes) and constitutional law (the fifth amendment of the US constitution demands "just compensation" for public takings of private property and "due process" before anyone is deprived of "life, liberty, or property"). Indeed, just about everyone agrees that judges inevitably employ moral reasoning to adjudicate some legal disputes. What theorists disagree about is how to explain this phenomenon.

Dworkin developed two related lines of criticisms against legal positivism based on this important aspect of legal reasoning. First, it's not obvious whether positivists can accommodate the way that moral principles inform the discovery

---

[20] 161 A2.d 69 (NJ 1960).   [21] Id. at 86.   [22] 22 NE 188 (NY 1889).   [23] Id. at 190.

of legal content – that is, their specific function or role in judicial reasoning that aims at law-discovery (1986a: pp. 20–35). The process of legal discovery does not involve a mechanical or algorithmic application of moral values to situations, by reference, say, to a set of instructions consisting of clear conditions of application and precise outcomes. In fact, as every competent lawyer knows, it's very difficult to predict, *ex ante*, the impact moral considerations have on judicial determinations concerning the content of the law. Dworkin argued based on such facts that the content and deliberative significance of moral principles cannot be captured in terms of the kinds of rules that are grounded in social practice and behavior, and so moral principles must be an independent ground of law.

Second, Dworkin (1986a: p. 24) pointed out that even if socially grounded rules or principles implicit in customs could, in theory, function as moral principles do in their contribution to legal reasoning, judges don't seem to derive their moral conclusions from social facts or customary rules. Instead, they simply *intuit* situations a certain way – as either just or unjust, reasonable or unreasonable – and factor these intuitions into their legal decisions. Furthermore, in cases like *Henningsen* and *Riggs*, it isn't clear that there were any socially accepted rules – say, a custom of disallowing murderers from inheriting under a victim's will – from which a judge could have derived the necessary conclusions. As Dworkin puts it, instead of invoking "a particular decision of some legislature or court," judges in such cases have relied on a "a sense of appropriateness developed in the profession." This strand of the overall argument questions whether a positivist account of the role of moral considerations in legal practice is consistent with what judges, in fact, say and do.

In response to the first challenge, positivists have endeavored to show that socially embraced rules and conventional norms can, in principle, function as moral principles do in modern adjudication (Berman 2022). I shall grant for the sake of argument that this response succeeds, that it is at least possible that judges who appear to be reasoning about what is just or fair are, in fact, trying to discern and apply some socially embraced rule (e.g., a rule whose content is fixed by what most people *believe* to be fair, rather than what is, in fact, fair). The present focus is on Dworkin's second line of argument which seems to me to be the stronger one – namely, that judges don't behave as if they are deriving their moral conclusions from socially embraced rules or conventions in the relevant range of cases; instead, they seem to be relying on their own sense of what justice and fairness require.

Positivists have offered several different responses to this second challenge. Some maintain that Dworkin overstated the significance of moral reasoning in adjudication, especially adjudication that involves law-*discovery*. When judges rely on moral considerations to decide a case, they take on the role of quasi-legislators, inventing new law rather than discovering pre-existing law (see, e.g., Marmor 2011: p. 66). Indeed, some forms of law-making by judges may be expressly permitted by local legal conventions or rules of recognition. One glaring problem with this account is that it doesn't seem consistent with the official view of participants within legal practice: judges for the most part don't characterize what they are doing as making up new law whenever they rely on moral principles, a point I'll come back to shortly.

Other positivists emphasize a distinction between law, or the grounds of law, and the tools judges use to discern the law. The fact that judges rely on moral considerations to reach legal conclusions is not a sufficient basis for inferring that the content of the law must be determined by moral facts, for moral considerations could simply be a convenient means of figuring out the nonmoral grounds of law given some correlation between the two. To illustrate, suppose that in cases like *Riggs*, the law of wills was determined, fully and without remainder, by the social facts concerning the legislature's overall secret preferences in relation to enforcement. It might still make sense for a court to engage in moral reasoning to figure out the legislature's preference, on the assumption that legislatures are in general morally motivated. On this interpretation, moral facts turn out to be *evidence* of what the law is, or of the law-determining social facts concerning legislative intent, but aren't, on their own, an independent source of law. More generally, it is worth noting that judges rely on all kinds of extra-legal rules and principles in adjudication as tools for figuring out the law – principles of logic, grammar, statistics, and, indeed, morality – and so, one cannot infer from adjudicative reliance alone that the relevant principles are law or grounds of law (Raz 1994: ch. 9, Shapiro 2011: p. 272).

Finally, some positivists – self-described "inclusive positivists" – grant that Dworkin successfully demonstrated that moral principles could have the status of law and serve as grounds of law (Waluchow 1994; Coleman 2001; Kramer 2004). But they insist that when moral principles have this status, it is always in virtue of contingent and jurisdiction-specific legal rules – specifically, more fundamental rules of law within the system whose legality is grounded in social facts alone. For instance, an enacted statue or constitution might direct judges to rely on moral considerations to decide cases, or a socially embraced rule of recognition might designate moral principles as a source of law.[24] However, inclusive positivists maintain that while "moral principles *can* enter ... into any particular society's law (as criteria for legal validity or as legal norms)" they "*need* not enter" (Kramer 2004: p. 245). The legality of a moral principle within

---

[24] Marmor (2004b: pp. 9–11) helpfully distinguishes these different ways moral principles might get into the law on the inclusive positivist picture.

some legal system cannot be established based on a priori reflection on the nature and concept of law alone.[25] The flaw in Dworkin's reasoning, we're told, is the inference from a contingent and local phenomenon – the status of moral principles within American and English common law – to a general conclusion that moral principles *necessarily* determine the law even in jurisdictions that lack the relevant social permissions and directives derived from more fundamental positive laws.

These responses, despite being mutually inconsistent, may seem persuasive when the phenomenon Dworkin drew attention to is studied in isolation from the broader historical context. Indeed, Dworkin focused quite narrowly on a small selection of illustrative cases from a distinctive legal system that confers an unusual amount of authority on judges. But as discussed previously in 2.1, for much of legal history and across a broad range of legal systems, jurists didn't simply *rely* on principles that they deemed moral or rational to reach downstream legal conclusions; they explicitly classified such principles as a form of a priori law of trans-jurisdictional scope. Contemporary jurists rarely endorse such claims explicitly. But the historical background renders positivist explanations of contemporary practice less plausible for several reasons. First, the role of moral principles in legal reasoning seems anything but peripheral in view of the larger context. Second, unlike rules of grammar or logic, moral principles have been explicitly classified as a form of law in manifestly juridical contexts. Third, contemporary judges who rely on moral principles to decide cases often defer to prior judges on the explanation of why such reliance is appropriate, at times explicitly.[26] And if such chains of deference hold, then contemporary practice may well take for granted, to some extent, prior accounts of the status of moral principles within law, accounts that are incompatible with positivism. At the very least, modern adjudicative behavior appears related to, and may be rationalized by, historical assumptions about the status of moral principles, which strengthens the case for taking those assumptions seriously.

At any rate, we have reasons for seeking a more unifying explanation of the role of moral principles within legal systems, especially given that there appears to be no consensus among positivists about how contemporary legal practice ought to be understood. This lack of consensus is, I think, telling. The various explanations, considered individually and independently of the historical facts,

---

[25] This is one of several important claims that sets inclusive positivism apart from the form of non-positivism that I ultimately defend in this volume. Nevertheless, there are similarities between the two views along with important differences that I shall discuss in Section 3.

[26] See, e.g., the dissent in *State v Joyner*, 625 A(2d) 791 (Conn. 1993) at 814, noting approvingly that a commitment to natural law "pervaded eighteenth century legal thought throughout America, including Connecticut." See Postema (2018: p. 37) for the importance of trans-historical deference within the common law.

don't fit the observed behavioral facts perfectly and involve contestable assumptions. It's not clear, for instance, that the rules found in customs and conventions can capture the content of moral principles or that judges are reasoning about specifically *social* facts when they reason about justice. It is also unclear whether and to what extent there *are* social permissions in the relevant jurisdictions to reason as the court did in *Riggs*, reasoning that the dissent explicitly deemed inconsistent with the role of the judge as defined by the American legal tradition (more on the significance of disagreement shortly). Even if moral principles *could* be law, or a source of law, simply because judges treat them as law (a social fact), the problem is that judges disagree about morality – its content – as well as about the legality of moral principles. Again, *Riggs* is a good case for illustrating the lack of juridical consensus, but similar disagreements crop up in the context of, say constitutional law and interpretation (Dworkin 1996). These problems with the positivist line suggest that, at a minimum, we shouldn't settle for a positivist explanation before evaluating competing non-positivist explanations of judicial behavior, which we'll consider in Section 3.

2.3 Persistent Theoretical Disagreement

Dworkin (1986b: ch. 1) mined other aspects of legal reasoning for insights into law's nature. One regular feature is the persistence among legal experts of what Dworkin called "theoretical disagreement." An ordinary disagreement between two officials might concern the content of the law – whether this or that rule counts as a legal rule within the jurisdiction. Theoretical disagreements, by contrast, concern the grounds or determinants of the law – the so-called "criteria of legality" (p. 4). To illustrate, some constitutional originalists in the United States believe that constitutional law is determined by the meaning of the constitution's text at the time of the constitution's ratification. Meanwhile, non-originalists insist that what the text might mean today as well as nonsemantic facts concerning, say, the public's preferences or sound public policy determine the law. This disagreement between originalists and non-originalists isn't simply about the content of American constitutional law but rather about what determines its content.[27] A striking fact about such disagreements is that they don't seem to turn on the content of any specific laws within the jurisdiction, such as customary laws of interpretation.[28] Nor do they appear to be semantic in nature, concerning the meaning of "law." Most importantly, theoretical disagreements don't seem to be cases of *talking past* – that is, the disagreeing parties appear to be disagreeing about a shared subject matter

---

[27] See discussion in Solum (2015).
[28] For an opposing and unconventional take on the originalism debate, see Baude and Sachs (2019).

(Shapiro 2007). There are questions about how often such disagreements occur, and how much theoretical disagreement is possible within a legal system (Leiter 2009, 2019; cf. Ewing 2017; Smith 2010).[29] But everyone agrees that the phenomenon is sufficiently regular to demand an explanation.

The explanatory challenge for positivists is easily illustrated using Hart's view. Recall that according to Hart, the laws of a jurisdiction derive from higher-order rules of recognition and adjudication that are embraced by legal officials. But theoretical disagreements suggest a lack of consensus among officials about the content of any such rules. Judges who embrace competing theories of constitutional law, for instance, don't agree on the law-determining facts, the jurisdiction's criteria of legal validity. So, if Hart's view is correct, then judges in these situations appear to be systematically mistaken, at least insofar as their claims about the law-determining facts outstrip the agreed-upon content of any higher-order rules. To illustrate, a rule of recognition in the United State won't settle the question of whether originalism or non-originalism offers the correct account of the determinants of American constitutional law simply because there isn't anything resembling consensus on this issue among legal officials, whether measured in terms of their beliefs or practical dispositions.[30]

In fact, the problem isn't just that Hartian positivism entails that judges and other legal officials must be mistaken about the law-determining facts within their jurisdiction (so that positivism turns out not to be neutral on substantive questions of legal content about which experts disagree). The problem is the implication that officials who persist in theoretical disagreements must be systematically and pervasively confused about the nature of law and legality. For surely, these officials are aware of a remarkable lack of consensus concerning the subject matter of their disagreement. And so, they must not realize that social convergence on a rule of recognition determines the law. Insofar as positivism entails an error theory about ordinary legal practice in the sense that some opposing and mistaken philosophy of law pervades and regulates legal practice, positivists owe us an explanation of why legal experts end up

---

[29] The question of the limits of theoretical disagreement within a functioning legal system is underdiscussed. Could a competent American jurist deny that acts of congress make American law or the intra-systemic superiority of the US constitution? In fact, there are plenty of people (both liberal and conservative) who think that the US constitution is *not* the supreme law of the land in the United States. Nevertheless, the conceptual space for disagreement is probably more constrained than non-positivists like to admit. See Watson (2023).

[30] Some positivists maintain that there can be multiple, inconsistent rules of recognition, driven by consensus within smaller groups of officials (Raz 1979: pp. 95–96; Gardner 2012: pp. 1–6). But that doesn't solve the puzzle about disagreement, since it's unclear why these groups take themselves to be right and opposing groups wrong about an alleged matter of fact: the intra-systemic grounds of law.

mistaken in these ways about the category – that is, they owe us a *theory* of error.³¹

Of course, an error theory about theoretical disagreements turns out not to be the only option if we're willing to look past surface appearances – that is, the claims of legal officials taken at face value. Perhaps their claims are simply disingenuous or amount to a kind of pretense (Leiter 2009; Marmor 2010; Plunkett & Sundell 2013). Watson (2023: p. 1), for instance, accuses Dworkin of construing judicial speech too literally, and writes that:

> If we pay attention to the pragmatics of judicial speech, we see that judges do not disagree over what the grounds of law are; they at most disagree over how courts should proceed when agreed-upon, though imprecise, grounds of law underdetermine what the content of the law directs in the case at hand.

Unfortunately, positivists rarely offer much evidence in favor of this interpretation and others like it, which is surprising given their concession that the behavioral evidence taken at face value cuts against the interpretation. Watson acknowledges that "judges nearly always speak as if there *is* a fact of the matter" about the grounds of law, and "they speak this way even when it is obvious that legal texts' meanings or holdings do not fully determine what legal content directs" (p. 20; cf. Leiter 2009: p. 1223). Although some judges do make positivist-friendly claims that involve acknowledging, say, their willingness to fill "gaps," the point is that many don't, a fact that invites explanation. Such facts are usually explained away by appeal to psychological or political factors, such as a strongly felt need on the part of judges to hide the inconvenient fact that their decisions outstrip pre-determined rules of law (Marmor 2010: p. 66). But judges who engage in theoretical disagreements seem awfully sincere. And their alleged disingenuousness does not come to light through, for example, admissions in other (private or nonlegal) contexts, admissions that would count as actual evidence for the positivist line. So, the bottom line is that we need more evidence.

By now, a recurring theme should not escape notice. Embracing legal positivism entails viewing legal experts in a rather uncharitable light: core participants in legal practice are either systematically mistaken or disingenuous. The theory might still be correct, of course. But its imperfect fit with both historical and contemporary judicial practice suggests that the theoretical core of positivism may not be doing much explanatory work when it comes to the regular and perplexing features of legal systems. An apt comparison might be a scientific theory that regularly

---

³¹ It is generally agreed that philosophical error theories about ordinary practice bear a theoretical burden of explaining, either in terms of the theory or ancillary commitments, why participants in the practice end up systematically mistaken. For discussion, see Hirsch (2002: p. 116), Korman (2009), and Kovacs (2019).

explains away inconsistent observations as experimental error. The inconsistencies between ordinary practice and positivism justify, I submit, exploring alternative theories of law, especially those that endeavor to understand ordinary legal practice more charitably. Indeed, the case against positivism so far is incomplete since it turns, ultimately, on a comparative evaluation of the theoretical virtues and vices of competing non-positivist explanations of legal practice. For now, the point is just that certain salient features of legal practice lack straightforward explanations if legal positivism is true.

Before moving on to other desiderata, it might be helpful to briefly compare the argument from theoretical disagreement to an analogous argument in a different area of philosophy: metaethics. The comparison is, I think, revealing. It is often argued that an adequate philosophical account of the moral domain needs to explain radical moral disagreement. People can diverge radically in terms of what they regard as morally right or wrong, good or bad, and yet still count as disagreeing about a shared subject matter (Horgan & Timmons 1991). In this regard, moral terms behave very differently from natural kind terms like "water." The point is sometimes motivated using a scenario dubbed "Moral Twin Earth" involving "Twin Earthlings" who are much like us except that they regard as good what we regard as bad, and vice versa. Despite this radical disagreement about the *extension* of the concept of the good, it is tempting to think that our counterparts on Twin Earth disagree with us about the good as long as their concept plays the same functional role in their motivational psychology as ours: we're all motivated to pursue what we judge to be good (and avoid what we judge to be bad). Natural kind concepts, such as the concept of water, don't seem to work this way: when linguistic communities radically diverge on the extension of "water," it counts as evidence that they employ distinct concepts.

The lesson that some metaethicists draw from such thought experiments is that what fixes the meaning of moral terms, and, correspondingly, the criteria for conceptual competence, isn't extensional judgments, rather it must be something like a term's functional role. Likewise, Dworkin's argument from theoretical disagreement appeals to a meta-semantic intuition – namely, that theoretical legal disagreements are *genuine* disagreements about a shared subject (the grounds of law), even if parties endorse radically different claims about legal content and its grounds. What this suggests is that, as in the normative case, conceptual competence isn't defined by knowledge of a precise extension for LAW, or strict application criteria, but something else. Perhaps functional-role facts are central here as well. In any case, the concept of law exhibits similar features as moral concepts which points to a potential connection, and even if legal disagreements can't be as radical (in terms of extensional conflict) as their moral analogues, a point we shall return to in Section 3.

2.4 Variations on the Gunman Situation (or the Problem of the Legal Borderline)

So far, we've approached the adequacy of positivism indirectly. We've considered some facts about law that seem difficult to explain if positivism is true, such as the persistence of theoretical disagreement among legal experts, and the treatment of moral principles by ordinary legal officials and their historical counterparts. But the force of such considerations depends, ultimately, on whether non-positivist views can better explain the highlighted facts without incurring significant theoretical costs (a question we'll turn to in Sections 3 and 4). The challenge so far has thus been conditional. What follows is a more direct challenge to positivism based on the plausibility of its extensional implications – that is, the theory's classification of certain schemes of social organization as systems of law.

Consider a scenario that one might describe, using Hart's (1994: p. 19) famous phrase, as "the gunman situation writ large." A criminal organization gains complete control of a state's coercive and administrative apparatus. The organization establishes rules expressly designed to transfer wealth and resources from the general population to its leadership. Moreover, the organization does so with impunity, having made its self-regarding goals and ambitions explicit. Municipalities and local authorities are afforded some room to govern, but any rules these subordinate institutions establish must be consistent with the supreme imperatives of the organizational leadership, directing the population to serve and enrich the lives of the ruling class. We can stipulate that the citizens more or less comply with these rules, given the credible threat of ruthless sanctions. Moreover, imagine that this criminal organization is sufficiently sophisticated to have established a social order that exhibits higher-order structure. There are rules for determining the content of the primary rules that govern, say, tax-and-transfer, as well as rules for changing the primary rules, though these higher-order rules are also established for the sole purpose of efficiently exploiting the public.

Do the rules established by our imagined tyrants constitute a legal system? It is at least tempting to suppose otherwise. The explicit and sole function of the system is to benefit those in power, and the system attracts compliance only because the populace is terrified. Of course, many legal regimes over the course of human history have been both extractive and coercive. But such regimes have at least tried to offer some justifying narrative. They've paid lip service to higher ideals than pure self-interest, such as, divine right or resistance against external (and even more vicious) oppressors and bogeymen. Even when extractive rulers have claimed that the powerful, simply in virtue of having power, have the right to rule, their claims have been manifestly *normative* – that might makes *right*. By contrast, the situation we've described involves unapologetically nihilistic robbers and thieves who admit to serving no one but themselves. Hart rightly questioned any account of the nature of law that would confer the status of legality on this picture of pure coercion. His principal target was Austin's brand of positivism, according to which law *just is* the commands issued by a "sovereign" who happens to be habitually obeyed because she credibly threatens sanction. Austinian positivists would have no problem calling the criminal organization's system of rules a form of law, whereas many positivists and non-positivists have felt, quite naturally I think, that although it might resemble a legal system, it is too openly exploitative to count as one, to be elevated, that is, to the status of law and legality.

Hart believed that what's missing from the gunman situation is genuinely felt obligation on the part of officials and the populace. Of course, there is a sense in which the terrified citizens feel obliged to comply – namely, out of concern for their own safety. But the existence of a legal system depends, Hart argued, on officials and others taking what he called the "internal point of view," embracing the rules as, in some sense, *worthy* of obedience. In our hypothetical, neither the tyrants running the show nor the citizenry speak in the characteristic language of morality of what *ought* to be done, of what's justified, obligatory, or permissible when describing their rules. According to Hart, this is the reason why the "gunman situation writ large" falls short of legality.

To avoid the Austinian implications, other positivists have proposed other supplementary criteria as essential to law that aren't satisfied in the gunman situation. For instance, Raz (1994: ch. 9) maintains that law necessarily claims authority over its subjects. On a standard construal of Raz's authority thesis, the claim of authority is supposed to be (a) a normative claim – a claim of genuine or legitimate authority, not just raw power; and (b) endorsed by officials and other key members of the legal system.[32] Along similar lines, Shapiro (2011) has argued that to ensure extensional adequacy, positivists should acknowledge that law, necessarily, has a moral aim – roughly, that of promoting the general good – whether or not it actually achieves that aim. As with Raz's authority thesis, Shapiro's moral aim thesis is standardly interpreted in terms of representations and assumptions made by the officials of a legal system (Plunkett 2013). So, perhaps what's missing in the case of the radically criminal organization

---

[32] For Raz, genuine or legitimate authorities issue directives that when followed by their subjects enable those subjects to conform to what they have independent reason to do better than if the subjects tried to figure out the directive-independent reasons for themselves. His concept of authority is thus a manifestly normative notion.

exercising its coercive powers is simply a claim to legitimate authority or, relatedly, other-regarding and more broadly moral motives.

But the extensional challenge to positivism inspired by the gunman situation can be strengthened in ways that undermine the diagnosis offered by Hart and his followers. Suppose that the criminals in charge in our imagined scenario are deeply confused. In addition to being highly self-regarding and cruel, they are mistaken about morality's demands. The gunmen believe that radical selfishness pursued at all costs is what justice requires, and accordingly, cast their self-interested commands to the wider populace in the language of morality – specifically, in terms of the allegedly self-evident truth that self-interest, ruthlessly pursued, is good. It's not at all clear that we've suddenly succeeded in imagining a legal system based on this slight alteration to the original hypothetical, which shows, I think, that the failure of officials to *claim* authority or to *represent* a social order as aiming at what they sincerely believe to be right and good is not a sufficient explanation for why the "gunman situation writ large" fails to deliver a legal system.

In fact, we can develop a range of potential counterexamples to legal positivism inspired by Hart's challenge to Austin. In addition to the moralizing yet egoistic tyrants, we can imagine tyrants who have absurdist moral commitments. These particular gunmen impose entirely arbitrary duties on the wider population. They enact rules requiring bizarre and pointless acts in one-off situations targeting specifically named individuals. Their rules apply retroactively, criminalizing choices made prior to the rule's enactment. To make matters worse, the organization's rules change several times each day. In short, the organization establishes a system of rules that isn't just arbitrary and pointless but one that regularly flouts all of the characteristics that Lon Fuller famously argued are constitutive virtues of law, such as generality, clarity, stability, and nonretroactivity, virtues that plausibly make the law good *as* a system of *law* (cf. Fuller 1978: ch. 2).[33] As before, the organization elicits nontrivial compliance through credible threats, and the terrified populace does its best to conform. Moreover, we can stipulate that the leaders genuinely believe that compliance with the rules is morally required. Yet it isn't clear that our absurdist tyrants are running a *legal* system or a system of *law*. A social order that is entirely and utterly arbitrary lacks the semblance of legality.

Here's a more qualified way of putting the point. What's missing in the highlighted examples, I submit, is a *clear* semblance of legality. The situations we've described are *hard* cases in the sense that it's not obvious whether the social orders count as systems of law, a lack of obviousness that's borne out by empirical

---

[33] For further discussion of Fuller's point, see 2.5.

research on laypeople's intuitions about laws and legal systems (Flanagan & Hannikainen 2020). Accordingly, a good account of the nature of law should be able to explain *why* such cases seem hard (Atiq 2020a: p. 21). This fact can be acknowledged without embracing any controversial non-positivist assumptions about law's essential goodness (e.g., that law is, necessarily, worthy of respect, or that it essentially gives its subjects strong, even decisive, moral reasons for legal compliance; cf. Finnis 2011; Murphy 2005). Even if positivists want to insist, ultimately, that there *can* be radically selfish and tyrannical legal systems, or morally mistaken systems of law composed of entirely arbitrary rules, they need to explain, in terms of their theory and/or any ancillary commitments, why such systems fall on the fuzzy edge of legality.[34] And that's not the same as explaining why the social orders count as immoral, irrational, or, even, simply unfamiliar. For things can be good or bad in ways that don't tell against (or in favor of) kind-membership. A weapon used in war might be highly immoral or unusual and yet count as a paradigmatic example of an instrument of war. The explanatory challenge involves saying why the moral badness or irrationality of law seems connected in some way to questions of classification – that is, to whether a scheme of social organization counts as a *legal* order. That is, perhaps, the least question-begging way of characterizing the argument based on the various "gunman situations." For as we shall see in Section 3, non-positivists face an analogous explanatory burden associated with evil or arbitrary law.

The options for revising positivism to explain the legal borderline seem limited. Positivism is constrained, by design, in the kinds of facts it can appeal to as potential grounds of law, or criteria of legality. The grounds and criteria must be non-normative in nature. For instance, Hart's claim that legal systems are, essentially, hierarchical systems of rules is a claim about the formal, non-normative features that law necessarily instantiates. One might hope that by further specifying some such non-normative conditions on the existence of a legal system, positivists might discover resources for distinguishing hard from easy cases of legality. Indeed, law's hierarchical structure was not the only formal feature that Hart emphasized in his theory of law. In an intriguing yet somewhat opaque passage, Hart (1958: p. 619) mentions that only rules of more or less *general* application can constitute a legal system.[35] He derives the generality constraint from the very idea of a rule, which, according to Hart, has

---

[34] Finnis (2011) makes a related though distinct point when he notes that a theory of law should have the resources to explain why some instances of law are "central cases" and others peripheral. What I'm emphasizing here (and have elsewhere) is an *epistemic* fact that invites explanation: the fact that it is intuitively unclear how we should classify these various nonstandard or unfamiliar cases (Atiq 2019: pp. 119–121; Atiq 2020a: fn. 53).

[35] Notably, Hart's discussion of generality appears in the context of his response to a point owing to Fuller (1978), who famously argued that not just generality but various other features, like

the generality requirement baked into it. In fact, Hart's claim that a rule, by its very nature, cannot be overly specific in its content (turning, say, on some person's identity or some one-off situation) is eminently questionable. But we can set the truth or falsity of his theory of rules aside. The point is simply to illustrate how a non-normative feature, insofar as it is essential to law, might constrain how arbitrary or absurd a legal system can possibly be.

This approach to the problem seems unlikely to succeed for several reasons. First, the kinds of structural features of law that positivists have historically emphasized fail to explain why the various gunman situations involve borderline cases of law at best. Certainly, the essential generality of law does not, on its own, rule out the emergence of what is manifestly a legal system out of explicitly selfish, absurd, and moralizing tyranny.[36] Second and more importantly, the more formal or non-normative features we treat as *essential* to law, the more complicated our positivist account of law becomes. And for any such non-normative feature that's alleged to be essential to law, positivists owe us an explanation of *why* it is essential (consider Hart's explanation of generality in terms of the nature of rules). And the explanation cannot simply be that it helps positivists avoid the potential counter-examples. Otherwise, the resulting strain of positivism will seem gerrymandered to solve an extensional problem that positivists uniquely face. The borderline cases we've discussed thus involve complicating the standard positivist story in ways that positivists have yet to address.

My own view is that the classification of the various gunman scenarios should not be a starting point for a theory of law (cf. Finnis 1980: pp. 9–11). Since it's not obvious what we should say about such cases – a fact we should all admit on either intuitive grounds or on the basis of an inference from peer disagreement (see Atiq 2019: pp. 119–121) – we may need to leave the problem posed by our conflicting extensional intuitions unresolved, for now, and return to it after we've examined our reasoning about laws and legal systems more broadly. Our broader commitments in the philosophy of law might help us address the problem. And that is precisely how I intend to proceed in the remainder of this section and the next, by exploring what light we can shed on our uncertainty – the fact that we don't quite know what to say about the legal borderline – by investigating other legal matters, such as the underdiscussed fact that law is susceptible to kind-relative evaluation.

---

clarity, publicity, and nonretroactivity, are, in some sense, essential to law (cf. Waldron 2008b; Raz 2019). We shall return to this Fullerian theme shortly.

[36] Moreover, if the essential features of law are described in irreducibly normative terms, such as nonarbitrariness, impartiality, or fairness, then the view begins to look a lot like non-positivism (see 2.5). In fact, some positivists have suggested that even Raz's authority thesis and Shapiro's moral aim thesis go a step too far in the direction of non-positivism (Plunkett 2013).

2.5 Law as an Artifactual, Functional, and Goodness-Fixing Kind

The argument of this section requires some setup, and, specifically, some discussion of our ordinary ways of evaluating things.[37] We can evaluate things as good or bad, better or worse, relative to different criteria. A knife might be evaluated for how well it cuts things, its beauty, cost, and a range of other features. But sometimes the criteria we use to evaluate things seem nonaccidentally connected to the kind of thing it is. In the case of knives, it's natural to think that the better a knife is at cutting things the better it is qua *knife*, whereas any analogous claim about a knife's beauty or cost would seem confusing and artificial. We mark this distinction in ordinary language in several different ways. When we wish to indicate that the criteria of evaluation are kind-relative, we employ the idiom of being good *as a K* or qua *K*. The linguistic resources available to us for this purpose are in fact quite rich: we might say "*K*s, insofar as they are *K*s, are better if they are *G* ...," "*K*s, as such, should be *G* ...," "inasmuch as something is a *K* ...," "what is a *K* is to that extent ...," and so on.[38] Additionally, kind-relative standards of evaluation are associated with certain modal and classificatory judgments. For example, it is tempting to suppose that necessarily, any object that counts as a knife must be, to some extent, good at cutting things; and, moreover, that being able to cut things well would make a knife good *as a knife* in any possible scenario, whereas it needn't make the knife good all things considered or in some kind-independent (e.g., moral) sense.

Judy Thomson (2008) famously described such kinds as "goodness-fixing," whose nature she argued fixes a (restricted) standard for evaluating instances as better or worse. Not all kinds are goodness-fixing. It makes little sense to ask what makes a rock good *as a rock*, and the same goes for colors, numbers, sets and collections. But examples of goodness-fixing kinds are easily multiplied (consider hearts, clocks, and poems) and can be drawn from a variety of different domains (the biological, artifactual, and aesthetic). Indeed, some philosophers (including Thomson) think that understanding such kinds – that is, why they are goodness-fixing – is the key to understanding normativity (cf. Geach 1956; Foot 2001; Smith 2013). But we needn't go that far.[39]

What's relevant for our purposes is the remarkable consensus within legal philosophy that *law* is a goodness-fixing kind. Both positivists and nonpositivists seem to agree that certain features make the law better *as law* (Atiq

---

[37] This section summarizes and builds on an argument in Atiq (forthcoming). As I explain at the end of the section, the argument is strengthened by our extensional considerations in 2.4.

[38] I rely here on Barney's (2023) observations concerning the ubiquity of "qua-predication."

[39] For a critical view to which I'm broadly sympathetic, see, e.g., Scanlon (forthcoming).

forthcoming: pp. 1–2). The relevant good-making features include clarity (whether a law's content is clear), generality (whether the law applies to groups of peoples and types of situations, rather than named individuals or one-off events), publicity (both in terms of the content of the law and the reasons for it), and nonretroactivity (the inapplicability of law to events that occurred prior to its enactment). Lon Fuller (1978) described such features as capturing the "inner morality of law," and the contemporary literature, following Raz (1979, 2019), refers to them as "the Rule-of-Law virtues." That they are widely regarded as kind-relative or constitutive virtues of law is evident from the fact that legal philosophers employ the standard idiom of kind-relative evaluation ("being good/better as *K*") and endorse modal and classificatory judgments generally associated with goodness-fixing kinds. For instance, Raz (2019) writes that "the rule of law" consists of a set of characteristics that together represent "the specific virtue of the law *as law*, a *universal* doctrine applying to *all* legal systems" (see also Kramer 2007: ch. 3; Marmor 2004a: p. 10; Murphy 2006; Shapiro 2011: p. 391).

Since this relative consensus will serve as the basis for a case against positivism, it is worth asking whether the consensus extends beyond legal philosophy – whether, say, the layperson on the street is used to thinking of law as evaluable *as law*. I suspect it takes some reflection to warm up to the idea. Nevertheless (and contrary to my armchair expectations), some recent experimental work suggests that even laypeople consider the features of laws highlighted by Fuller and others (like generality and publicity) to be in some sense "essential to the law" in that all legal systems *ought* to instantiate the relevant features to some extent, "even though actual laws routinely violate them" (Hannikainen et al. 2021).

An argument in defense of the claim that law is a goodness-fixing kind appeals to law's artifactual and functional nature (cf. Moore 1992, Murphy 2006, Crowe 2019).[40] Artifacts are intentional creations or products of purposive agency. In addition to physical or concrete artifacts, such as clocks and knives, there are, also, abstract artifacts, such as symphonies, novels, computer programs, and, indeed, law.[41] Again, this is a point of relative consensus (Leiter 2011: p. 666). Moreover, it is tempting to think of law as a functional artifact, the kind of artifact that serves some salient function or set of functions. Unsurprisingly, a wide range

---

[40] Natural lawyers argue that the *moral* merits of law are kind-relative merits. I'll discuss their arguments in detail in Section 3.1. This section is focused, exclusively, on a critique of positivism based on a weak claim that even positivists by and large concede – namely, that the Rule of Law defines a kind-relative standard for evaluating law.

[41] This distinction between concrete and abstract artifacts, though not relevant to the argument of this section, will matter later in Section 3.

of functions have historically been attributed to law, such as coordination between agents, dispute settlement, or the promotion of societal welfare (Ehrenberg 2016: p. 182). The basis for such function-attributions requires some discussion. But the initial and hopefully uncontroversial point is just that functional artifacts, such as knives, guns, computer programs, and universities, tend to be goodness-fixing.

It is worth examining this relationship more closely. A popular view in the literature is that it is precisely the functions of artifacts that define a restricted (kind-relative) standard for evaluating instances (cf. Thomson 2008). Not just any function, mind you, but an *essential* or *constitutive* function.[42] To use a well-worn example, someone's intention to create or use a physical object *for the purpose of cutting things* partly explains why the object counts as a knife (if it does). Knives can be used for many purposes besides cutting things (e.g., as decorative objects), and there is a sense of "function" that tracks even one-off uses to which an object might be put (e.g., being used as a toothpick). But cutting things is plausibly essential to our *concept* of a knife, or our concept of what it takes for something to be a knife. And this function – not just any old use to which a knife might be put – explains the constitutive virtue of knives: being good at cutting things. Likewise, what makes a flat-head screwdriver good *as a screwdriver* is its effectiveness at turning screws, and not, say, prying things open, even if its frequently used to pry things open.

Like others writing in this area, I take the connection between artifacts, essential functions, and kind-relative evaluation to be implicit in ordinary thought and talk. But it would be a mistake to pretend that these issues are settled, and I shouldn't be misconstrued as suggesting that they are. How we should understand function attributions, not just in social theory but in biology and the natural sciences (where talk of functions is pervasive), is philosophically contested (see, e.g., Cummins 1975; Wright 1973; Millikan 1984). And the same is true of kind-relative evaluation (cf. Scanlon forthcoming). What this means is that any explanation of law's nature as a goodness-fixing kind will necessarily involve broader commitments in metaphysics and meta-normative theory. Nevertheless, there is a basis for thinking that once we clarify these broader commitments, the right framework for thinking about these issues puts considerable pressure on positivist theories of law.

To illustrate, suppose we take for granted, as many do, that an artifact's kind-relative virtues are explained by essential functions. The challenge in the legal case is: (1) to specify a suitable function, (2) explain why law has the function essentially or constitutively, and (3) explain how this essential function relates

---
[42] As discussed in Section 1, I shall rely on an account of the essential properties of abstract objects defended by Zalta (2006), among others.

to the classic Rule-of-Law virtues. A familiar source of essential functions for artifacts lies in the agency of creators and sustainers.[43] Since law and legal institutions are the product of *collective* agency, any shared intention one might appeal to would have to be extremely general and nonspecific. For example, we cannot assume that legal systems essentially involve agents intending to adopt a body of rules that are designed to be (1) clear, (2) general, (3) nonretroactive, and so on, where the entire list of Rule-of-Law features show up explicitly in the shared intention to create law. Fuller (1964: p. 146) puts the point nicely when he observes:

> There is an intrinsic improbability about any theory that attempts to write *purpose* in a large hand over a whole institution. Institutions are constituted of a multitude of individual human actions. Many of these follow grooves of habit and can hardly be said to be purposive at all. Of those that are purposive, the objectives sought by the actors are of the most diverse nature. Even those who participate in the creation of institutions may have very different views of the purpose or function of the institutions they bring into being.

Our functionalist thesis about law thus needs to be a "modest and sober one."

Fuller's own view was that law's essential function is to "subject conduct to the guidance of rules" (38–57). But his view doesn't quite explain why the classic Rule-of-Law features define a kind-relative standard for evaluating laws. One glaring problem with the proposal is that highly specific laws – say, rules that impose one-off obligations on named individuals – can guide people's conduct perfectly well. In fact, an entire system of rules can be pervasively specific, with different rules for each person, and yet succeed in guiding conduct. Another problem is that not every feature, or set of features, that causally contribute(s) to an artifact's ability to perform its essential function counts as a kind-relative virtue. This is because causal connections can be contingent whereas kind-relative virtues appear to be modally general, perhaps even necessary. So, even if the law's instantiation of features like publicity causally contribute to law's ability to guide conduct in ordinary scenarios, that doesn't result in the kind of explanation we are after, one that's true in a range of

---

[43] For a recent development of an intentionalist/agentive model for explaining artifactual functions, see, Evnine (2016). The intentionalist model does not explain function-talk in biology very well. On an alternative nonagentive "etiological" model, kind-functions are identified with whatever performance explains the emergence and proliferation of instances of the kind in environments characterized by various selection pressures (see, e.g., Wright 1973). I am not aware of a systematic application of a "pure" (i.e., entirely nonagentive) etiological account to explain kind-relative virtues and our ordinary evaluative-talk, in particular. That said, the argument of this section may be compatible with such an account, although the argument's success would then turn on the empirical question of what explains the persistence and proliferation of legal systems, and whether a discovered etiological function can adequately explain the Rule of Law.

possible scenarios involving law, including, say, a dystopian scenario where subjects are guided by radically nonpublic law due to microchips implanted by the authorities in their brains, which receive regular "over-the-air" updates as the law changes.[44]

The most plausible candidate for an essential function of law that is both (a) plausibly grounded in the shared intentions that produce law *and* (b) can explain the specific ingredients of the Rule of Law, is a *normative* function (Atiq forthcoming: pp. 17–18). On this view, legal rules are, essentially, rules that are accepted (chosen, enforced, followed ...) as N, where N is some very general normative property (such as the property of being *reasonable* or *admirable* or *fair*). Only a normative ideal, insofar as its realization is law's essential function, could bear the right sort of constitutive (i.e., noncausal and modally robust) connection to specific Rule-of-Law characteristics, such as publicity and generality. Consider, for instance, a recent suggestion owing to Peter Railton (2019) that communities committed to formal rules of social cooperation systematically care about ideals of interpersonal fairness to some extent (see also Simmonds 2008: ch. 6; Pettit 2023: ch. 2).[45] An ideal of interpersonal fairness does seem suitably tied to specific Rule-of-Law features, given that laws that are radically specific or nonpublic or retroactive, and so on, seem contrary to some such ideal and necessarily so. By contrast, it is very hard to think of some non-normative property that might be similarly related to the specific Rule-of-Law features – that is, noncausally and constitutively related.

So far, none of this begs any questions against the positivist. It isn't question-begging to assume that the existence of law depends on the social acceptance of rules based on some normative assumptions. On the contrary, we observed earlier that a number of positivists have defended specific versions of our more general assumption (e.g., Raz's authority thesis, Shapiro's moral aim thesis, and Hart's claim that the existence of law depends on officials adopting the "internal point of view"). Moreover, as we discussed in 2.4, positivists may need to embrace some such commitment in order to avoid counterintuitive

---

[44] For a detailed discussion of various other problems with Fuller's proposal and related positivist accounts such as Marmor's (2007), see Atiq (forthcoming: pp. 14–16). Cf. Raz (2019: pp. 4–5, 14). One response to the objection raised above involves supplementing Fuller's account with an ideal of *rational* guidance: law aims to guide its subjects through their powers of reason. But this revision to the Fullerian view brings us much closer to the essentially normative view I am about to defend, where law's function is the realization of a limited normative ideal.

[45] Simmonds (2008: ch. 1), drawing on Kant, argues that the Rule of Law embodies "an intrinsically valuable form of moral association," because it creates certain spheres of freedom and independence that wouldn't be possible without it. For our purposes, we needn't choose between competing accounts of the nature of the ideal. Our present goal has been to motivate the thesis that the realization of some distinctive normative ideal is law's essential function and to draw out the implications of this functional thesis.

extensional implications. What we've presently discovered is that the commitment finds further justification in the explanatory work it can do for us regarding law's susceptibility to kind-relative evaluation.

The challenge for positivism emerges once we draw out the implications of the theoretical assumptions we've relied on. Our explanation for why law is a goodness-fixing kind treats law as a functional artifact. And instances of such kinds appear to be subject to what Kathryn Lindeman (2017) calls the "threshold requirement." To be an instance of such a kind, an object must be minimally good at performing the kind-relative function, where the threshold of sufficiency is indeterminate. To illustrate, a radically blunt piece of scrap metal can fail to be a knife, despite the good intentions of an incompetent designer, and the way in which it fails is noncausal and functional: the failure concerns *what it is* to be a knife. The threshold requirement is not just intuitive, it finds confirmation in leading philosophical theories of the nature of artifacts (both concrete and abstract).[46] Hence, no account of what grounds the existence of some instance of an artifactual kind could be complete that didn't refer to the instance's minimally adequate performance of the kind-function. If law is an unexceptional artifact, as we've assumed throughout, then for a social order to count as law it must be minimally good at realizing law's normative function. And this fact entails that law's existence must be grounded in its normative merits after all, albeit to some underspecified and minimal degree.

As far as I can tell, positivists have had very little to say about this challenge. They might insist that law, unlike other functional artifacts that are goodness-fixing, isn't subject to the threshold condition (cf. Shapiro 2011: p. 392),[47] or that law's kind-relative virtues can be explained in some other, nonstandard way (cf. Raz 2019).[48] But absent an explanation of *why* law should be so

---

[46] See, e.g., Thomasson's (2003: p. 600, 2007: p. 59), Hilpinen (1993: p. 161), and discussion in Atiq (forthcoming: pp. 10–12).

[47] Shapiro maintains that "it is part of the nature of law to have a moral aim" but denies that "the failure to attain this end undermines the law's identity as law." He points out (rightly) that "a defective instance of a kind is not ipso facto an attenuated version of the kind." Defective instances can certainly be full-fledged members of a kind. However, Shapiro overlooks the fact that *radical* defects can and do interfere with kind-membership. Ordinary examples of the phenomenon are easily multiplied. I intend to produce a knife but due to incompetence and lack of knowledge, my productive efforts result in a useless piece of scrap metal. What I produce is not a knife because it falls so radically short of the function of knives. Why shouldn't the same be true of law qua functional kind? Notably, Shapiro doesn't motivate his claims based on a general theory of functional and goodness-fixing kinds, and a key point of this section is precisely that our claims about the relationship between law's nature, function, and existence conditions are less ad hoc when located within a general and independently motivated theory.

[48] As I argue elsewhere (Atiq forthcoming), Raz's (1979, 2019) explanation of the Rule of Law is questionable precisely because it portrays law as an oddly exceptional goodness-fixing kind. However, Raz was acutely aware of the difficulties facing the traditional explanations offered by positivists, especially in his later writings and unlike other writers on the Rule of Law.

exceptional, any such move will seem ad hoc. To reiterate, we've leveraged an analogy with functional artifacts to explain a feature of law that needs explaining. Following the argument where it leads – that is, accepting the consequences of treating law as a functional artifact whose normative function explains its kind-relative virtues – entails accepting a minimal role for normative facts in the existence and grounding of legal systems.

Since this final argument is somewhat complex, it might be worth summarizing its key premises:

(1) The fact that law is susceptible to kind-relative evaluation in terms of the specific Rule-of-Law features (generality, publicity, ...) invites explanation.
(2) What likely explains law's susceptibility to kind-relative evaluation in (1) is the fact that law is a functional artifact.
(3) For the explanation in (2) to work, we must appeal to an essential function that's both (a) plausibly intended whenever communities come together to create and run a legal system, and (b) constitutively tied to the Rule-of-Law features,
(4) The only essential function that satisfies the criteria in (3) is some normative function: the realization of some limited normative ideal (related, say, to interpersonal fairness).
(5) If law has a normative function (as per (4)), then it's being minimally good at that function – that is, its realization of the relevant normative ideal to some extent – is a condition and ground of law's existence, since all functional artifacts are subject to such conditions.

As I've already acknowledged, several premises rely on assumptions about functional kinds and kind-relative evaluation that, though independently motivated, are not irresistible. Positivists might be tempted to reject some of the background metaphysics. But it requires defending an alternative theory that positivists have yet to develop. Notably, an attractive upshot of the argument is that it nicely explains why we struggled to classify the kinds of social orders we encountered in 2.4. If it is an essential truth about law that law must be to some extent reasonable or fair but the relevant threshold is indeterminate, then it isn't surprising that the legality of the radically unfair and unreasonable social orders we encountered previously seemed unclear.

***

Let us summarize the overall case against positivism. Positivists struggle to explain several regular and striking features of legal systems and legal reasoning, including: (1) the traditional classification of moral principles as a form of a priori law; (2) the role of such principles in legal discovery by contemporary judges; (3) persistent theoretical (or higher-order) disagreement among jurists about the law-determining facts within their legal system; (4) the fact that radically arbitrary or immoral schemes of social organization represent, at best, borderline cases of legal systems; and (5) the fact that law appears to be a goodness-fixing kind whose kind-relative virtues plausibly derive from its artifactual and functional nature. I haven't claimed that positivist-friendly explanations of the highlighted phenomena are impossible or inconceivable; rather, I've argued that the theory's explanatory power is questionable given that the available explanations seem undermotivated and rely on ancillary commitments that are less than fully satisfying. For instance, positivist explanations involve uncharitable interpretation (legal officials are systematically mistaken or confused), improbable assumptions (the category of law is historically discontinuous), and ad hoc rejections of general explanatory frameworks (law is exceptional as a goodness-fixing kind). That said, a theory isn't defeated by explanatory gaps, baroqueness, or, even, a few counterintuitive implications. The question is whether there are alternative, non-positivist theories that do better at meeting our desiderata and without incurring new theoretical costs that outweigh any gains. That is the question we now turn to.

3 How to Be a Legal Non-Positivist

We began our discussion with an intuitive, even commonsensical, positivist paradigm for understanding law and legal orders. For all its simplicity, the paradigm struggled to explain some non-obvious legal phenomena that it takes a degree of immersion in legal history and practice to recognize. While positivists believe these problems to be solvable within the framework of their theory, different positivists have offered different solutions and have, correspondingly, revised the theory in different ways. But the proposed solutions are less than fully satisfying, which may explain the lack of consensus among defenders on how the theory's explanatory gaps should be resolved.

These theoretical challenges warrant exploring alternative paradigms. In this section, the focus is on non-positivist theories of law and legal orders. Since non-positivism is a very broad tent, the accounts we're about to discuss might seem unrelated in their ontologies, methodology, and explanatory focus. Nevertheless, I'll try to motivate some surprising connections by the end of the discussion. I'll start by introducing some prominent varieties of non-positivism. We'll consider how these theories address the explanatory demands raised in the previous section as well as some of the unique challenges they raise. With the mainstream views on the table, I'll make a case for combining the insights captured by different versions of non-positivism, while avoiding some of the more extravagant postulates, to reveal a moderate position that accommodates the desiderata without departing too radically from positivistic starting points.

3.1 Natural Law Theories, Strong and Weak

Recall that for much of legal history, the official account of the content of law embraced by jurists included references to "natural law," conceived as a set of moral and rational principles exhibiting self-evident or a priori legality – that is, legality in virtue of content alone. In practice, the natural law sometimes functioned as a set of default rules, filling gaps in "positive" law, and sometimes as supreme or "higher law," which so-called positive law could not violate (2.1). Natural law *theories* are perhaps best viewed in the light of this historical context. They include relatively free-standing commitments in ethics and metaethics, concerning the nature of moral norms, the content of the common good, and the principles of right action, as well as commitments in the philosophy of law.[49] In what follows, I shall focus primarily, though not exclusively, on the legal philosophy of natural law theorists, though it warrants emphasis that the existence of objective principles of practical rationality and morality serves as a starting point for these theorists.[50] Different natural law theorists flesh out the content of the relevant principles differently. And there are, likewise, different accounts of the metaphysics, including both secular and religious accounts of the grounds. But the idea that there are some such principles, whose normative significance and deliberative importance makes them categorically unlike socially constructed norms, such as the rules of etiquette, games, or language, serves as common ground.

Aquinas' view may be the most widely discussed natural law theory. Legal rules, according to Aquinas, represent a socially mediated concretization of the general moral principles that govern agents. As he famously put it, law is an "ordinance of reason ... issued by one who has care of the community and promulgated."[51] Why do moral principles require socially mediated concretization? Aquinas maintains with considerable plausibility that many such principles have an abstract form: they prescribe or prohibit general types of actions (e.g., "no unreasonable risks" or "help the disadvantaged") and, consequently, can be satisfied in different ways. Positive law, when enacted by an appropriate agent motivated by concern for the common good, converts these general principles of

---

[49] See, e.g., Finnis (1980: pp. 86–90, 2011: p. 12). We shall return to metaethics and its relevance to legal philosophy in Section 4.
[50] For an overview of natural-law moral theory, see Murphy (2001).
[51] Summa Theologiae Part Ia IIae 90.

morality into determinate and more precise requirements.[52] Partly because law gives specific content to, and is a means of complying with, general moral imperatives, it has comparable normative force: it gives its subjects genuine and often decisive reasons for compliance (cf. Murphy 2006; Finnis 2011).

Aquinas' view has exerted a powerful influence on contemporary natural law theorists, but it is widely acknowledged that his central claim was less than precise. The claim that law "is an ordinance of reason" has been interpreted in at least two ways, corresponding, roughly, to the "is" of identity and the "is" of predication (Murphy 2005). The "strong natural law thesis," which interprets the claim as an identity statement, entirely excludes unjust or unreasonable rules from the category of law (p. 19). This view is hard to maintain given how easy it is to multiply examples of wicked, unjust, or otherwise unreasonable laws and legal systems (cf. Finnis 1980). On an alternative and more popular interpretation, the "weak natural law thesis," Aquinas takes consistency with practical reason to be a regular (or "generic") feature of law,[53] one that's sufficiently regular to define a constitutive standard for evaluating laws without ruling out the possibility of unreasonable laws (Murphy 2006: p. 21). That is, when the law departs from the true moral principles, law's unreasonableness amounts to a distinctly *legal* defect, a way of being defective *as law*. Recall our observation in 2.4 that many ordinary kinds are associated with kind-relative or constitutive standards for evaluating instances. The weak natural law thesis amounts to the view that law isn't just some ordinary goodness-fixing kind; its constitutive or kind-relative virtues include such properties as *being morally justified*.

The weak natural law thesis plausibly entails some version of the strong. As discussed previously, the existence and persistence of goodness-fixing kinds seems subject to a threshold condition – instances must exhibit kind-specific virtues to some, albeit underspecified, degree to count as members of the kind (2.5). Hence, if the weak natural law thesis is true, then although *mere* unreasonableness or wickedness may not preclude a social order from counting as a legal system, *radical* unreasonableness and wickedness might. Proponents of the weak natural law thesis often acknowledge as much.[54] But this connection between the weak and strong

---

[52] Summa Theologiae Part Ia IIae 96.
[53] On this interpretation, Aquinas' claim that law is an ordinance of reason amounts to a generic claim like "tigers are striped." An initial problem for this interpretation is that Aquinas is also famous for the paradoxical-sounding thesis that an "unjust law is not law." As we'll discuss shortly, there turns out to be a connection between the strong and the weak natural law theses.
[54] Crowe (2019: p. 181) writes: "A poorly drafted, unjust or unreasonable standard will be legally defective, while an incomprehensible or deeply repugnant standard may be no law at all." Similar endorsements of the claim that legality is inconsistent with radical injustice that reaches "an intolerable level" can be found in Alexy (1999: p. 16), Radbruch (1973), and Soper (2007). For a helpful discussion of the relationship between kind-relative defectiveness conditions and existence conditions, see Murphy (2012: pp. 59–60).

theses is worth emphasizing because positivists sometimes struggle to see how the weak thesis puts any pressure on their view. Both theses involve giving up, albeit to varying degrees, a core positivist assumption – namely, that the existence of laws and legal systems does not ultimately depend on moral facts and can be fully explained without having to rely on a substantive theory of what morality demands.

In either form, natural law theory confronts two central challenges. One is metaethical: the need to explain and motivate the existence of objective principles of morality that float freely from the beliefs and preferences of agents. I will return to this challenge in Section 4, as it deserves an extended discussion since a commitment to some form of moral realism may turn out to be the main theoretical cost of non-positivism.

The second challenge is meta-legal: it involves motivating the claim that law, unlike other systems of socially dependent norms, bears the proposed connection to what's morally or rationally required. Of course, part of the case will be based on considerations of explanatory power and an inference to the best explanation: that is, some natural law hypothesis may be necessary for accommodating the desiderata discussed in Section 2 (a point I shall return to in a moment). But more specifically, if the weak natural law thesis is true, we should be able to explain why *being morally justified* makes the law good *as law*, ideally in terms of an independently motivated theory of goodness-fixing kinds. Natural law theorists thus face a stronger version of the explanatory challenge discussed in 2.4. For the idea that law's kind-relative virtues include moral goodness is considerably more controversial and, it seems fair to say, nonobvious than any corresponding claim about the classic Rule-of-Law features, such as generality, nonretroactivity, and publicity (cf. Marmor 2004a; Waldron 2008b).

Natural law theorists have responded to the meta-legal challenge in various ways. On Finnis' (2011: pp. 9–11, 2007) view, moral justification (or conformity with the true principles of morality) defines a kind-relative standard for evaluating law because paradigmatic instances of law – so-called "central cases" – exhibit such justifiability. Finnis maintains that all philosophical theorizing about kinds must start with uncontroversial instances, whose regular features invite explanation, and that the central and paradigmatic cases of law regularly promote the common good. Both claims are controversial. But even if they were true, Finnis doesn't explain why only some regular features of central cases but not others define kind-relative standards of evaluation (on this point, see Murphy 2012: pp. 50–51). It is a regular feature of paradigmatic law that it consists of rules directed at imperfect, uncooperative human beings, and, so, includes highly coercive and punitive measures. But that fact does not bear any obvious connection to law's constitutive virtues. It is not as though law is better qua law if it is highly coercive/punitive, for we can imagine good law in a society of angels (or even a society of better-than-average beings) that isn't all that punitive (cf. Raz 1999: p. 159).[55] So, the question of why law's moral virtues make it good *as law* remains unanswered, even if we accept Finnis' point about the significance of central cases to philosophical theorizing about kinds.

An alternative and more popular approach to explaining why the moral merits of law might be constitutive merits treats law as a functional kind. On this approach, a kind's constitutive virtues are characteristics that make instances better at performing the kind's essential function(s). Murphy (2005, 2006) explores two types of functional explanations for the weak natural law thesis, developing themes he finds in Moore (1992) and Alexy (2010a). The first explains a kind's essential function in terms of some "characteristic" performance by its instances. Whether a function is "characteristically" performed depends on "not just statistical frequency" but frequency relative to "normal" background conditions (2005: pp. 26–27). Elsewhere, I have expressed doubts about any such account of function-attribution especially insofar as we want functions to explain constitutive virtues (Atiq forthcoming: pp. 14–15). To take an ordinary counterexample, a statistically dominant use of flathead screwdrivers around the house is prying things open, and that's true in normal conditions since most screws are Philips-head. But prying things open is not the constitutive function of flathead screwdrivers; nor does it define a kind-relative standard for evaluating instances. What makes a *good* flat-head screwdriver in the relevant sense of "good" is, plainly, effectiveness at turning flathead screws. The corresponding claim about usefulness for prying things open (that it makes the screwdriver good *as a flathead screwdriver*") sounds artificial. Put differently, not all "characteristic functions" in Muphy's sense are essential or virtue-defining functions.

In any case, based on his theory of function-attribution, Murphy (2005: p. 26) argues that the characteristic function of law is "to lay down norms with which agents will have sufficient [moral] reason to comply." Murphy (2006: ch. 3, 2012) offers an additional argument in support of his claim about law's essential function. This alternative argument relies on the idea that the law consists, essentially, of speech acts that involve various demands. We're told that the law's specific demands – for example, "drive on the right!" – implicitly claim (or presuppose) that subjects have decisive reasons to comply (cf. Alexy 1999). Murphy maintains that such speech acts are defective *as demands* when their content and presuppositions are false. Relatedly, law is defective *as law* (i.e., as a system of norms making various demands on agents) when it fails to give

---

[55] Raz relies on the "society of angels" scenario to show that coercion isn't essential to law. My point here is that coerciveness is also not one of law's constitutive virtues, even though law is characteristically coercive.

agents decisive reasons for compliance. This view is vulnerable to several objections. For one, it's not obvious what justifies attributing to law (as opposed to, say, legal officials) any implicit claims, especially, the kinds of claims that interest the natural lawyer – namely, that there are decisive *moral* reasons for complying with the law. Moreover, claims and assertions can be insincere. In such cases, the falsity of what's represented as being the case needn't render the speech act defective *as a speech act* given the speaker's goals, though of course the act might be morally criticizable or defective in some other kind-independent sense. Indeed, Murphy's crucial claim that "lying and bullshitting are intrinsically flawed forms of asserting, defective *in their kind*" seems to me to stand in need of greater defense.[56]

Even if we were to grant the natural lawyer's claims about law's function, whether based on some characteristic performance or speech act theory, the view confronts a very basic problem. It doesn't explain why key ingredients of the Rule of Law, like generality and publicity, count as constitutive virtues of law. Highly specific rules informing named individuals how to act in one-off situations can give agents "decisive reasons to comply," at least when backed by the threat of sanction. That is, a pervasively nongeneral system of laws seems perfectly capable of performing law's alleged function. Even in the absence of coercive threats, it's at least conceivable that there might be moral reasons to comply with highly particular norms.[57] So, Murphy's account of law's function does not explain why generality is a constitutive legal virtue. This result is in a way unsurprising because explaining the Rule of Law is not the principal aim of natural law theorists. But the point is precisely that the explanation is necessary. In general, the functions of functional kinds explain paradigmatic kind-relative virtues (see 2.5). And so, a theory of law as a functional kind should be evaluated for how well it explains the relatively uncontroversial constitutive virtues of law like generality, nonretroactivity, and publicity – that is, the core of the Rule of Law about which positivists, non-positivists, ordinary jurists, and laypersons seem to agree. Unless it meets this basic criterion of adequacy, the theory, along with its implications regarding less

---

[56] Similarly, Robert Alexy (2021: ch. 3) argues that law necessarily claims moral "correctness" and the claim's falsity renders law defective. Alexy considers the objection that law's claim may be "nothing more than an expression of an illusion or an error." But his response is, to put it frankly, obscure. As far as I can tell, there is no real discussion of the possibility that if I don't intend a sincere speech act, it's content being false needn't render it defective as a speech act. For further discussion of the importance of sincerity in the productive intentions that bear on kind-relative evaluation, see Atiq (forthcoming: 20–21).

[57] If moral particularism is true, then there are no general, exceptionless principles that determine the rightness or wrongness of actions in particular situations. See, e.g., Dancy (2004).

obvious constitutive legal virtues such as justice or reasonableness, will seem suspect.

Consider, finally, a more recent attempt by Crowe (2019: p. 218) to ground law's essential function in "authorial intentions and social acceptance," a style of explanation that works well in the case of created artifacts with intended functions. Crowe suggests that given the intentions of the primary authors and subjects of legal systems, the essential function of law is to be "generally regarded by members of the community as conferring obligations" (p. 174). Additionally, Crowe maintains that the injustice or irrationality of a law renders it defective qua law by undermining its effectiveness at generating a robust sense of obligation amongst persons. As I've argued elsewhere, it's unclear how a weak natural law thesis is supposed to follow from this functional thesis, given that unreasonable laws might be, and often are, extremely effective at generating a sense of obligation in an unreasonable community (Atiq 2020b). That is, it won't always be true (or true in every community) that the moral merits of law make the law effective at performing its alleged function. However, it's tempting to suppose that kind-relative virtues are virtues of the kind in a broad range of actual and possible scenarios. To illustrate, in any situation where we find knives, being able to cut things well makes the knife good *as a knife*. A functional explanation of law's kind-relative virtues should thus modally generalize, but Crowe's does not.

The above criticisms notwithstanding, these proposals exhibit the right general form to explain why law is a goodness-fixing kind. For reasons highlighted in 2.4, if law is a functional kind with some normative function – a function derived, perhaps, from the intentional social activities that produce law – it would plausibly explain our ability to evaluate law as law. And so, the problems I've raised above may only arise for specific versions of natural law theory, a point I shall return to shortly.

For now, consider how such theories fare in terms of addressing other explanatory demands introduced in Section 2. On the one hand, they seem tailormade to explain why radically wicked or unreasonable social orders challenge our legal classificatory judgments. It's difficult to classify such social orders not just because they are atypical but because of a general fact about goodness-fixing kinds, including knives, clocks, poems, and, indeed, law. Genuine instances of such kinds must perform their kind-relevant function well to some degree, though it's very hard to specify a precise threshold (2.4). In the case of law, the relevant function is securing justice and reasonableness, and so it is hard to know precisely how unjust or unreasonable a social order can be before it fails to qualify as a legal order.

On the other hand, it's less clear how natural law theory explains aspects of legal reasoning highlighted by Dworkin and others. Consider the classification of principles such as *nemo iudex in causa sua* as a source of law or, even, as a priori law. The moral defects of law may be *legal* defects, or make the law defective *as law*, but why should that entail the a priori legality of any moral or rational principle? This seems to me to be a symptom of a larger problem: it isn't clear how the strong and weak natural law theses relate to the classification of individual rules and principles under the concept of law. Natural law theorists have traditionally focused on law as an institution, or on what makes an entire system of rules a legal order, while being relatively less concerned with articulating general "criteria of legal validity" for specific rules or principles within legal systems. But we employ the concept of law to refer to both systems of rules and specific rules of law, such as those derived from statutes or court decisions. Presumably, there is some connection between these two ways of using the category.

One possibility is that natural law theory can simply absorb what Hart (or any other positivist) says about the social criteria of legality (e.g., derivability from the customary rule of recognition), albeit subject to a moral constraint on the existence of a legal order.[58] But then the theory risks inheriting the problems Hart faces in relation, say, to theoretical disagreement (more on this in a moment). Alternatively, the theory might by supplemented with an independent account of adjudication that sheds light on the nature of legal reasoning (Finnis 2011; Crowe 2019). For instance, Crowe (2019: p. 196) argues that a judge's role in interpreting law is to "interpret legal materials in such a way as to render them non-defective as law." As a consequence, judges must be sensitive to law's purpose and function. If, *ex hypothesi*, all law constitutively aims at justice or the common good, and if judges are entitled to consider law's purpose in figuring out what the law is, we have the beginnings of an explanation for why moral principles might be regarded as a form of law: the content of such principles constrains the content of individual legal rules at least as formulated by judges.

Still, the proposal as sketched leaves several questions unanswered. Why assume that a judge's professional responsibility is to "improve" the law by making legal pronouncements which render the law "non-defective"? Why not embrace what seems to be the more standard view – that a judge's sole responsibility is to take a clear-eyed view on what the law is, no matter how defective it might be "as law" or in any other sense? Crowe's conception of the judge's role is controversial to say the least. Moreover, even if we assume that

---

[58] For discussion on this point, see Murphy (2005).

judges are entitled to take the overarching moral purpose of law into account in discovering specific laws, it isn't obvious why that would entitle jurists to declare moral principles a priori law even in the absence of formal promulgation (cf. Aquinas, *Summa Theologiae*).

Perhaps relatedly, it's not obvious whether natural law theory sheds enough light on a central feature of legal reasoning in complex legal systems – persistent theoretical disagreement – to constitute a sufficient advance on legal positivism. For even if law either essentially is or aspires to be an "ordinance of reason" (compatible, that is, with the requirements of reason and morality), it's unclear why jurists persistently disagree about the grounds of legality in full awareness of a lack of intra-systemic consensus on the question. Consider, for instance, a natural law theory that follows Hart in its specification of the social criteria of legality (derivability from the customary rule of recognition) while adding a moral threshold condition (which applies irrespective of the social facts). On the one hand, the "Hartian" natural lawyer can invoke explanatory resources that weren't available to Hart: some disagreements about the grounds of law persist because of persistent moral disagreement within the legal community about what justice, in fact, requires. On the other hand, the explanation seems incomplete since participants in theoretical legal disagreements often explicitly disavow moral motivations. Many constitutional originalists in the United States, for instance, maintain that their account of the grounds of constitutional law is motivated not by a sense that originalism entails morally good outcomes; rather, they claim to be motivated by a correct understanding of what law is and the judge's professional responsibility.[59] More generally, it seems that persons who agree on moral matters can, and often do, disagree about the grounds of law persistently and without conceptual confusion. So, there is more to the phenomenon that needs explaining. And since explaining theoretical disagreement plays such a central role in Ronald Dworkin's theory of law, perhaps that is where we should look next for insights into law's nature.

3.2 Dworkinian Interpretivism and the One-system View

Dworkin's (1986) account of law takes ordinary legal reasoning as its starting point and is expressly designed to accommodate the desiderata described in 2.2 and 2.3 – in particular, the role of moral principles in law discovery and persistent theoretical disagreement among jurists. Given its complexity, the account requires some setup.

Dworkin agreed with the positivist that legal facts (such as facts concerning a rule's legality or the existence of legal rights and obligations) depend on certain

---

[59] See, e.g., Baude and Sachs (2019).

nonmoral, social facts: roughly, facts concerning the actions of various institutions (e.g., a legislature or law-making body) and the desires and beliefs of agents operating within those institutions. The relevant social facts might include facts concerning the socially embraced rules of recognition, change, and the like. However, Dworkin maintained that any derivation of *law*, or legal rights and duties, from such social facts involves "interpretation" of institutional practice and, relying on his general theory of interpretation, defended a non-positivist metaphysics of law.

On Dworkin's view, whether one is interpreting a poem or a painting or indeed, the social practices that result in law, interpretation necessarily involves treating an object of interpretation (e.g., a set of sentences) as an instance of a normatively significant kind (e.g., a sonnet with aesthetic properties). Instances of normatively significant kinds can be ranked as better or worse based on kind-relative normative criteria. Moreover, the process of interpreting an object as an instance involves attributing meaning, purpose, and content to it "in order to make of it the best possible example of the form or genre to which it is taken to belong" (Dworkin 1986: p. 52). Interpretation is always constrained, to some extent, by the non-normative features of the object of interpretation. In the case of a sonnet, an interpretation must be responsive to the text, some range of meanings to which the terms and expressions are susceptible, and the intentions of the author – features Dworkin discussed under the rubric of a "dimension of fit." But a *good* interpretation imputes content that elevates the object of interpretation by representing it as a *good* instance of the relevant kind, and even if, for example, the imputed content cannot be located fully in the intentions of the agent(s) who produced the object. In the case of a sonnet, an interpretation that renders the sonnet more lovely but at the cost of fidelity to the intentions of its author might be superior to an interpretation constrained entirely by authorial intentions. Hence, evaluative considerations define a "dimension of justification" that, Dworkin argued, is an essential element of ideal interpretation.

In the case of legally relevant social practices, the normatively significant kind to which these practices allegedly belong (when imbued with legal content) is "a general justification for the exercise of state coercion" (1986a: p. 190). That is, the social facts interpreted as resulting in legal duties, rights, and responsibilities (including propositions of the form <the law requires that ...>) imply an explanation of why the state is justified in coercively enforcing its rules against its subjects. Naturally, this justification will be more or less plausible depending on the goodness or justice of legal rules and requirements. Moral principles, therefore, operate as a constraint on legal interpretation.[60] Dworkin maintained that morality constrains the interpretation

---

[60] On the relevant set of principles, including the master principle of integrity, see Dworkin (1986a: pp. 90–93).

of *any* action or aspect of institutional practice that produces law – including, for example, a prior precedent or judicial ruling. That is, any interpretation of what the law requires in any context must be evaluated for how well it contributes to the overall justification for the state's coercive authority.

Note that there is a way of construing Dworkin's claims in exclusively epistemic terms. What he offers is a heuristic for adjudication, an account of how judges should go about "discovering" law in light of social practice facts that doesn't necessarily track the law's metaphysics. However, any such construal would underestimate the radical nature of Dworkin's thesis. On the intended metaphysical construal, there is nothing more to legal facts – facts concerning, say, the *legality* of a rule – than facts concerning the best interpretation of social practice. The fact that the law obliges drivers to drive on the right is in some sense reducible to the fact that the best interpretation of what we do around here is that we expect and coercively enforce driving on the right. And the latter fact concerning the best interpretation is grounded in both non-normatively characterized social facts (the choices and intentions of institutional actors) and moral facts (our institutional practice is portrayed in a morally good light). Hence, legal facts are partly grounded in moral facts.

Like the natural law theorist, Dworkin conceives of legally relevant social practices as having a normative role: namely, as contributing to a case for justified state coercion. But his reasons are radically different. Dworkin is motivated by a certain conception of interpretation within legal practice and its metaphysical implications – that is, its implications concerning the nature of legal facts.[61] These reasons are the source of the view's distinct advantages but also some of its unique vulnerabilities.

Let's start with the advantages. The view straightforwardly explains why judges reach for moral principles when interpreting prior precedent and institutional practice. Judges engaged in interpretation are keen to cast the law in its morally best light, even if that means going beyond the manifest intentions and actions of agents. It was no accident, for example, that even though there was no prior judicial opinion or statute that would have prevented a murderer from inheriting under a victim's will in *Riggs v Palmer*, the court nevertheless held that principles of justice "constrain" what the law requires. It's less clear how Dworkin's view explains the historical treatment of moral principles as a priori law, but we can develop a plausible story for at least some such principles: moral principles, insofar as they operate as conceptual constraints on what the law could be, are akin to "laws of law." If, for example, law cannot permit largescale

---

[61] Dworkin differs also in his metaethics – in particular, his account of the nature of moral facts. See, e.g., Dworkin (2011). But we can ignore this difference for now. On Dworkin's metaethical quietism, see McGrath (2014).

torture and genocide (because no institutional practice that included such permissions would be justified in its coercive activity or worthy of obedience), then it seems fair to say that the fact that a genuine legal system does not permit largescale torture and genocide is appreciable a priori, and without regard to any specific facts about social practice.

Furthermore, Dworkin's view offers a nice explanation of persistent theoretical disagreement. It's possible that disagreements about the determinants of law are driven by persistent *moral* disagreement regarding what would justify state coercion. On this picture, constitutional originalists and non-originalists in the United States disagree about the grounds of American constitutional law precisely because they disagree about what legal content casts American law in its "morally best" light. However, as I suggested earlier, participants in these debates often don't view their disagreement as explained by moral disagreements. Theoretical legal disagreements seem to persist in the face of moral consensus. Fortunately, an alternative diagnosis falls out of Dworkin's view, one that relies on his central claim that the concept of law is an interpretive concept. In interpretive disagreements, what secures a shared subject matter is consensus regarding *the object* of interpretation, which in the legal case is a set of social practices. An interpreter might ignore moral considerations and the dimension of justification altogether when interpreting social practice, and although the resulting interpretation would not be a very good one, it would still count as an interpretation of the relevant subject. On this view of the disagreement between originalists and non-originalists, the originalist is portrayed as confused not about the social facts, morality, or, even, the concept of law[62] but about the nature of ideal interpretation.

Despite these explanatory advantages, the view is vulnerable to challenge on multiple fronts. Some critics have questioned Dworkin's theory of interpretation, charging him with overestimating the role of evaluative considerations in the interpretation of language and law (Marmor 2011, 2005). Since judges lack the expertise, time, and political authority to regularly engage in the kind of morally charged analysis Dworkin had in mind, both the empirical claim that they do pervasively and the normative claim that they ought to are questionable (Sunstein 1996).[63] A separate challenge stems from the fact that for a theory of law to be plausible, it needs to explain what sets legal norms apart from moral

---

[62] Perhaps all we need to know to be competent with the concept of law is certain uncontroversial extensional truths involving it along with the fact that the concept's application involves interpreting a legally relevant set of social practices. However, we needn't take a view, here, on what determines concept possession and concept mastery.

[63] It is no accident that Dworkin (1986: pp. 87–88) names his hypothetical judge who interprets the law correctly "Hercules." The task of making moral sense of social practice, including the entire legal history of a given jurisdiction, is, indeed, herculean.

norms, given that not every moral duty is legislated, enforced, or relied on by lawyers. Since Dworkin wasn't very precise on how considerations of fit and justification are balanced, the theory's extensional implications – its implications about the content of the law within jurisdictions – are hard to evaluate.[64] One relatively clear implication seems counterintuitive: the legal facts – that is, the content of the law within a jurisdiction – may be entirely inconsistent with subjects' beliefs about the law, since subjects who are morally mistaken may be radically cut off from the "morally best" interpretation of social practice (Raz 1985: p. 309; Marmor 2011: pp. 90–92).[65]

Recently, theorists who share Dworkin's emphasis on legal reasoning, though not necessarily his controversial account of interpretation, have argued that ordinary legal practice supports the view that legal norms are identical to a subset of moral norms (Greenberg 2014; Hershovitz 2023; Ryu 2024).[66] To illustrate based on Greenberg's (2014) development of the "one-system view," legal interpretation involves "moral reasoning about what is [morally] required as a consequence of ... relevant lawmaking actions," rather than reasoning about what would make an entire system of coercion "the best it can be" given the constraints of fit and justification (pp. 1303–1304). On this picture, legal requirements are supposed to be identical (or reducible) to those moral requirements (concerning, say, rights and responsibilities) that result from the actions of specific institutions. Nevertheless, what we morally should do *given institutional choices and actions* can be inferior to what we morally should do in an ideal institutional context, so there remains on this view a meaningful distinction between moral and legal norms (whether it is a sufficient distinction is debatable, however, as we'll discuss). Other defenders of the "one-system view" have explained the legally relevant subset of moral norms differently,

---

[64] On this point, see Finnis (1987).
[65] It's worth noting that Dworkin's view entails two kinds of radical legal error: (1) an entire community could fail to appreciate the legality of a norm; or (2) an entire community could wrongly take some norm to be law. I think the second upshot, emphasized by Marmor (2011, ch. 2), is more implausible than the first. See discussion in Atiq (2020a: pp. 23–24). Raz's (1985) critique of these implications of Dworkin's view is part of a more general critique based on the thesis that law necessarily aspires to be authoritative – that is, it purports to give subjects knowable peremptory reasons for action. Raz argues that free-standing moral principles are incapable of being directives, and insofar as their application involves moral reasoning, they cannot give subjects peremptory, content-independent reasons for action. But the claim that *all* laws must take the form of knowable and authoritative directives is highly suspect, as is the claim that legal imperatives cannot invite moral reflection from those who are subject to them. I suspect Raz mistakes generic truths about legal norms for necessary truths. For discussion on the peremptory status of legal directives and moral reasoning, see Kramer (2004: p. 23).
[66] Dworkin (2011: p. 403) seems to have favored a related thesis in his later work. On the continuity between Dworkin's interpretivism and the one-system view, see Nye (2021).

while sharing the core assumption that legal and moral norms form a single, unified body of norms.[67]

On what basis might one conclude that ordinary legal practice favors the "one-system" thesis? In several papers, Greenberg (2004, 2008) offers an intriguing argument. He argues that while social facts concerning, for example, the choices and intentions of legislatures play a role in determining the law, a core assumption of adjudicative practice (one he endorses) is that the law-determining social facts stand in a special relationship to facts concerning what the law is. Greenberg calls this relation "rational grounding." Roughly, the idea is that the legal facts (concerning what the law requires) must be *intelligible* given the law-determining social facts. "Intelligible" sounds like a normative notion. To say that the law is intelligible given the social facts in a jurisdiction sounds a lot like saying that there is something to be said *in favor* of the law given the social facts. But Greenberg expressly disavows the normative interpretation (pp. 190–191). He maintains that intelligibility means something like a priori accessibility: any rational agent who knows the law-determining social facts within the system should be able to derive, through a priori reflection – from the armchair, as it were – facts about legal rules, permissions, prohibitions, and so on.[68] But if positivism were true, then the legal facts *wouldn't* be derivable a priori from the social facts. The argument for this claim is subtle but turns primarily on the fact that the social facts – concerning people's behavior, customs, and so on – are always compatible with a range of competing rules or principles.[69] Legal positivism would have to be (surprisingly) some kind of a priori conceptual truth, Greenberg argues, for there to be anything like an a priori connection between legal content and the social facts. And quite apart from his critique of positivism, Greenberg suggests that the rational intelligibility of law favors the one-system of view. For many moral facts *are* derivable a priori from social facts – that is, what we morally ought to do, given the

---

[67] Hershovitz (2015, 2023: p. 192) seems to be moved by the thought that legal rules and obligations couldn't be "normative" in any sense besides the sense in which moral rules and obligations are normative. He suggests that of the moral obligations that qualify as legal obligations, some essentially depend on institutional choices, while others are simply moral obligations that are enforceable in court (Hershovitz 2015: pp. 1202–1203, 2023: pp. 84–91, 182–183).

[68] There might be other precisifications of Greenberg's somewhat elusive concept of "rational grounding." I think my interpretation renders the argument interesting and worthy of engagement. For an alternative take, see Chilovi and Pavlakos (2022).

[69] The reasons are related to Wittgenstein's puzzles about rule following (see Kripke 1982). To get a sense of the reasons, consider the history of your practice involving the rule for addition. Your behavior in adding up numbers is consistent with a rule of *quaddition*, which operates like addition but only for numbers up to some arbitrarily large number that you've never "added" before. For a similar point about social practice being compatible with many different legal rules, see Greenberg (2004: p. 182).

choices of people around us, seems knowable or understandable through rational reflection alone. So, if we assume that legal facts *just are* moral facts – that when judges reason about what law requires, they're reasoning about what morality requires (given the social facts) – it would explain the rational intelligibility of law.

The argument is complex, relies on contestable premises, and has been criticized on several fronts (see, e.g., Plunkett 2012, Neta 2004). One problem is that moral reasoning is not the only kind of normative reasoning that is arguably a priori; consider reasoning about what we prudentially ought to do given institutional choices. So, it isn't obvious why the argument favors a reduction of legal facts to specifically *moral* facts.[70] Additionally, Greenberg provides very little support for the claim that judicial practice assumes the rational intelligibility of law.[71] It's certainly not the case that jurists explicitly endorse any such general claim about law. Contrast, for instance, the willingness of legal officials to treat *select* principles of morality and rationality as "a priori law." Moreover, what *looks* like a priori reasoning within a domain is often, simply, reasoning based on implicit assumptions (assumptions concerning, say, the grounds of law or some bridge principle linking social facts to specific legal facts) that needn't be a priori true but can be taken for granted for a variety of reasons, such as being part of the common ground. Perceptual reasoning arguably operates this way. When I infer that I am currently in Ithaca, New York based on what I observe, I instinctively assume the falsity of various skeptical hypotheses that are neither inconsistent with my perceptual observations nor a priori false.

But perhaps the biggest worry about Greenberg's conclusions is that the inferred unity of law and morality is inconsistent with ordinary legal intuition: all-too-familiar legal obligations don't seem to correspond to moral obligations, whether construed as all-things-considered moral obligations or *pro tanto*. For instance, it seems natural to think that many legal officials were legally obliged

---

[70] To be fair, Greenberg acknowledges this possibility and explicitly invokes normative or value facts in the argument, rather than moral facts. But his ultimate view of the nature of legal facts, the moral impact theory, is cashed out in specifically moral terms.

[71] In a similar vein, Hershovitz (2023: p. 192) maintains that when legal actors make claims about legal rights and obligations in court, they make claims about who *morally* owes what to whom. Unfortunately, he offers scant evidence in support of this claim about ordinary legal practice. As far as I can tell, Hershovitz seems impressed mainly by the use of deontic and normative terminology in law and our practical goals in litigation. But we often speak in deontic terms – that is, in the language of obligation and right – without intending anything moral. Chess players might instruct a novice in terms of moves that ought to be made. That doesn't show that chess players intend a moral claim. In fact, Hershovitz acknowledges that ordinary legal actors routinely distinguish legal from moral obligation but insists that ordinary legal actors must be confused or speaking loosely (pp. 10–13, 109–111; cf. Hershovitz 2014: pp. 1191–1192).

to enforce the Fugitive Slave Act during the antebellum period in the United States, even though they weren't morally obliged (cf. Finnis 1980). Likewise, moral and legal obligations seem to come apart in various mundane and morally neutral cases. Dindjer (2020: p. 193) offers a nice illustration:

> Plausibly one very often has pro tanto obligations to comply with [traffic] rules. But it is difficult to imagine that, for every driver under all possible circumstances, this will be true – difficult to believe, for example, that, on an obviously deserted country road with no danger present, an experienced driver invariably violates a [moral] obligation in driving before the traffic lights have turned to green, or not indicating before a turn.

The kinds of moral considerations Greenberg and others invoke to explain obligations to obey the law in such cases – concerning, for instance, the importance of democracy, fairness, coordination, or the vindication of legitimate expectations – turn out to be far too limited in scope to guarantee a perfect correspondence between moral and (relatively trivial) legal obligations (p. 194).

Note that these objections based on the apparent divergence of legal and moral obligation do not beg any questions against the one-system theorist. We needn't assume that ordinary intuitions about law and obligation must be correct. The objection simply invites proponents of the one-system view to explain why widely shared intuitions of legality turn out to be mistaken. After all, we made similar demands of positivists. And unfortunately, a plausible error theory that can charitably explain why our legal intuitions might be systematically distorted in the highlighted cases does not fall out of the one-system view (see discussion in Atiq 2020a).

A related line of objections appeals to instances of widespread and uncomplicated legal agreement (Watson 2024, Leiter 2009: p. 1248). When practitioners of law reason about the consequences of, say, the statute of limitations, they don't generally deliberate on the moral question of how the statute affects what we – plaintiffs, defendants, judges, and others – should do. Instead, lawyers and judges apply the statute's bright-line rules specifying when claims can be brought to court very strictly. Yet, surely, it is extremely implausible to think that strict application of the statute of limitations in all cases is *morally required* (Watson 2024: pp. 75–76). More generally, Watson argues that if a view like Greenberg's were true, we would expect to see moral reasoning in legal practice far more often than we do. Recall that interpretivism was originally motivated, by Dworkin and others, based on an alleged consistency with ordinary legal practice, whereas the one-system view seems revisionary. And non-positivists cannot have it both ways: they cannot simultaneously insist that philosophers of law need to take the assumptions internal to legal practice seriously while disregarding inconsistencies as explanatorily irrelevant.

Ultimately, the question boils down to whether the theoretical benefits of moving from a positivist paradigm to a complex and more counterintuitive theory of law, such as interpretivism or the one-system view, outweigh the costs. Simpler and more commonsensical paradigms aren't always correct, of course. But it's far from clear that the explanatory gaps in, say, Hart's account of law warrant a paradigm shift as radical as the one proposed by Dworkin and his followers. Indeed, it is telling that the views we've discussed in this section take on commitments that don't appear to have a clear explanatory payoff. Consider, for instance, Dworkin's identification of the legal facts with facts concerning the best interpretation of social practice. Why, one wonders, is the law-entailing interpretation the *best* one – that is, the one that balances considerations of fit and justification "just right"? Why not think, instead, that interpretation in a more relaxed enterprise: that the legal facts reduce to facts concerning a "good enough" interpretation of social practice? After all, Dworkin invites us to take the analogy with literary theory seriously, where competing interpretations are often regarded as equally good (cf. Fish 1982).[72] Dworkin's reason for emphasizing a so-called "best" interpretation was his assumption that every legal question (such as the question of what prior precedent requires in a case) must have a uniquely correct answer, at least in principle (1986a: pp. 119–115). If interpretations need only be "good enough" – that is, balance considerations of fit and justification sufficiently well relative to some arbitrary threshold – to justify legal norms, there may not be a uniquely correct answer to every legal question. Inconsistent interpretations might satisfy the "good enough" threshold. But Dworkin did very little to justify his "one right answer" thesis, whether in terms of ordinary legal practice or the nature of interpretation more generally (Leiter 2004: p. 175; Kramer 2007b).

Nevertheless, there is much to learn from Dworkin's proposal and views inspired by it. Among other things, Dworkinian interpretivism suggests a promising recipe for explaining theoretical legal disagreement: appeal to a feature of the concept of law that ensures that individuals with radically different accounts of how social practices make law can genuinely, and without conceptual confusion, disagree about what the law is. As discussed earlier in the section on methodology, we need some understanding of the way the legal concept works, since we use it to fix a target of philosophical analysis. The

---

[72] Describing the debate between "intentionalists" and "anti-intentionalists" in literary interpretation, Kubala (2019: pp. 509–510) notes that "for the anti-intentionalist" there can be "a plurality of acceptable interpretations." The idea that there is one value-maximizing "super" interpretation seems to be a minority position in literary theory.

views we shall explore next take the nature of the ordinary concept and the rules governing its application as their primary focus.

3.3 Dual-Character and Aggregative-Cluster Concepts of Law

Natural law theorists and proponents of the "one-system" view lead with their metaphysics. Their starting point is a set of moral or legal facts. Even Dworkin, for all his emphasis on the *claims* about law made by officials and other participants in legal practice, was ultimately concerned with what those claims reveal about the nature and grounds of legal norms, construed as an objective reality, and not legal language per se. In fact, he derided what he took to be the overly semantic focus of certain forms of legal positivism (1986b: p. 46).

Some contemporary versions of non-positivism take legal language to be an important subject of investigation in its own right. If a non-positivist metaphysics of legal norms falls out of such views, it is not because clarifying the grounds of an objective order of norms is the motivating goal. Like Dworkin, proponents of such "language-first" views are especially concerned with explaining the nature and persistence of disagreement about law's relationship with morality. Their explanations proceed by way of a straightforwardly semantic (or meta-semantic) account of the ordinary concepts associated with legal terms and expressions.

One such account that has recently gained traction among philosophers engaged in the empirical study of legal language takes the ordinary concept of law to be a "dual character" concept (Flanagan & Hannikainen 2022; cf. Alexy 2010b). On a popular (though by no means uncontroversial) view in the philosophy of language, concepts are individuated by their application criteria. Dual character concepts are alleged to have "distinct criteria [of application], invoking concrete and abstract properties, respectively, that may yield opposed membership verdicts" (p. 168). Dual character structure has been proposed for concepts of social roles (DOCTOR, SCIENTIST) as well as concepts of artistic artifacts (PAINTING, NOVEL) (Knobe et al. 2013; Liao et al. 2020). The criteria for being a doctor might include passing a board exam or being licensed by an appropriate authority or obtaining a medical degree. But we often invoke more abstract and normative criteria to mark what makes someone a doctor in the unqualified or "full-fledged" sense. This is reflected in such ordinary claims as "only a licensed medical professional who desires to heal or help others qualifies as a *true* doctor" or "real doctors help people." In a recent study, Flanagan and Hannikainen (2022) found that laypersons seem to endorse analogous claims about law. When questioned about the legality of morally wicked rules in a hypothetical jurisdiction, participants in this study regularly distinguished morally wicked "laws" from "true laws," or laws in the full-fledged sense. Researchers have noted intriguingly consistent results across a range of legal cultures (Hannikainen et al. 2021). The phenomenon calls for an explanation, and Flanagan and Hannikainen argue that it is explained by dual-character structure: the legal concept's application criteria include both social and moral characteristics that yield inconsistent membership verdicts. Questions remain whether such studies are tracking *ordinary* claims about law as opposed to claims participants are only inclined to endorse when prompted by investigators.[73]

Other defenders of the dual character theory have relied on genealogical observations concerning the marked inconsistences in the way that legal language has been used over time. Almeida (2023) suggests that the historically contested status of the principles of morality within ordinary legal practice is explained by the dual character theory. He argues that for various sociological reasons, the salience of the two senses of the term "law" – the moral and the descriptive – has varied, and that this variance explains why earlier generations have considered certain principles of rationality or morality to be law in virtue of content alone, whereas analogous assumptions in moderns times are far more controversial. Relatedly, the dual character theory explains why our intuitions about legality are pulled in different directions when we encounter rules that satisfy only one of the two senses of the term. Similar classificatory puzzles can be generated using other dual character concepts: someone licensed to practice medicine but who intends to cause extreme harm to patients puts analogous pressure on the ordinary concept of a doctor.

Unfortunately, the dual character theory remains underdeveloped. We aren't told precisely how the social and moral senses of law relate. Dual character structure is supposed to be distinct from polysemy of the sort exhibited by words like "break" or "star." So, if there are two senses of the term "law," they presumably bear some relationship that ought to be clarified. Among other reasons, polysemy tends to be language-specific, whereas dual character structure is supposed to track some more general and cross-cultural feature or tendency in our cognitive scheme. One option for the dual character theorist is to lean on the account proponents of the one-system view give of the relationship between the moral and social conditions of legality: the moral condition, when satisfied, turns, in part, on the social condition. For instance, if legal rules must give agents moral reasons for compliance, the reasons may turn in part on the fact that law is a shared social commitment (cf. Ryu 2023). But this phenomenon doesn't generalize to other concepts that are supposed to exhibit dual-character structure, such as the concept of a doctor.

---

[73] See Plunkett and Philips (2023), who argue that the results might be driven not by dual meanings but contextual factors.

Another option would be to characterize the relationship between the moral and the social criteria of legality in terms of "aggregative clustering" (Atiq 2020a). Aggregative cluster concepts are concepts whose application involves an imprecise "aggregation" of distinct properties exhibited by members: an object falls under such a concept just in case it exemplifies to a sufficient (albeit imprecise) degree the associated properties (see Kovacs 2018; cf. Hedden & Nebel 2024). For instance, the concept RED applies to colors based on some combination of hue, chroma, and brightness, but the principle of combination is not precise enough to yield clear verdicts for every shade of color. More generally, aggregative cluster concepts are associated with clear and indeterminate instances. For instance, the concept BIGGER THAN applies to pairs of objects based on properties of volume, length, and mass. The ingredient properties can converge and result in easy comparisons, but they can also diverge in ways that lead to indeterminacy.[74] Nevertheless, concepts of redness and being bigger track objective similarities across members.

I have suggested in prior work that the concept of law may integrate in similarly imprecise yet principled ways the moral and social properties of rules.[75] Borrowing from Hart, suppose that the relevant social property is just the property of being a rule that's derivable from the rule of recognition embraced by a community from the internal point of view (i.e., with the requisite normative assumptions). The moral property might be the property of being a *good* or *just* rule. The key idea is to see these properties, when instantiated together, as determining a more complex and somewhat indeterminate property – perhaps the normative property of being sufficiently well-supported by a select class of reasons for following rules. One possibility is that legal actors weigh broadly "social" reasons for following rules as well as moral reasons in deciding whether a rule is sufficiently well-supported to count as law.[76] Rational agents regularly

---

[74] A rigorous statement of how the ingredient criteria of such "multi-dimensional concepts" are aggregated to yield overall judgments is beyond the scope of this volume. For problems and potential solutions, see Hedden and Nebel (forthcoming).

[75] One reviewer inquired why the "dual character" and "cluster concept" theories should be discussed together. The latter might seem related to Dworkin's interpretivism, especially in light of the question I pressed earlier against the interpretivist of why the legality of a rule should depend on the "best" interpretation of the social and moral facts as opposed to a "sufficiently good" interpretation. The cluster concept theory may be understood as a version of interpretivism with a fuzzy threshold of sufficiency. However, the main motivations for the theory – e.g., explaining inconsistent juridical intuitions about law, including intuitions that interpretivists dismiss as erroneous – differ from the motivations for Dworkin's interpretivism and are closer to the motivations for the dual character theory. See discussion in Atiq (2020a: pp. 19–21). To borrow an observation of Simon Blackburn's, often what matters in philosophy is not where we end up (our conclusions) but where we begin (e.g., what we set out to explain).

[76] Valenti (2024) argues that a distinctive reason to respect socially constructed norms is that doing so respects people's agency as reflected in their considered commitments. Valenti describes these reasons as "moral" in nature, but that's beside the point. The key idea for our purposes is that the cluster theory relies on different species of genuine reasons – e.g., Valenti's social reasons as well

weigh different kinds of reasons for action – including reasons that flow from our subjective attachments, such as special concern for a loved one or community conventions or one's life projects, as well as impartial, other-regarding moral considerations – in deciding whether a course of action is justified relative to the totality of their values. So, it's not implausible to think that legal actors might be doing something similar in the legal domain.

I confess to no longer being certain of the view's viability as described in prior work for reasons that will become clear shortly. I restate it here mainly to illustrate how the aggregative-cluster model might be applied to the concept of law, a point of some relevance to the discussion to follow, and to draw out its non-positivist implications. Both dual-character and aggregative-cluster accounts purport to identify, albeit at a very high level of generality, the rules for applying the legal concept *correctly* – that is, in ways that entail *true* claims of legality. On the dual character theory, a rule or body of rules must meet moral conditions to count as law in at least one ordinary sense of "law." Likewise, on the aggregative cluster model, whether the concept of law applies to some rule turns on its moral features. The relationship between such conceptual theses and a metaphysical thesis concerning the nature of *legality* – that is, the category that philosophers of law are interested in – is not straightforward.[77] One reason concerns our methodological observation from Section 1: the philosophy of law is not necessarily interested in all of the ways the ordinary concept of law might be employed; rather, the goal is to understand a sense of legality that is consistent with certain distinctions between social orders that become apparent upon reflection, and that can shed explanatory light on some very general phenomena associated with legal systems. So, the question remains whether the concept of law as characterized by the accounts we've discussed above can help us address our specific theoretical needs. As I'll explain shortly, there is some reason to think so. But for now, note that *if* a conceptual thesis of the sort discussed in this section turns out to be true, then it is extremely tempting to think that some facts of law in the ordinary sense of "law" are explained by facts of morality, at least in the same way that facts of bachelorhood are explained by facts concerning gender and marital status. The onus is on the positivist to explain why this implication, which seems prima facie inconsistent with positivism, would be philosophically irrelevant even if true.

---

as, say, impartial or welfarist reasons. The aggregative cluster concept of law thus tracks a complex normative property of rules *being sufficiently well-supported by a subset of normative reasons*, where the relevant subset defines a genuine, if partly indeterminate, normative ideal.

[77] See generally Smithson (2020), who distinguishes concept-grounding from kind- or property-grounding.

3.4 Non-positivism without the Frills

Can we distill from the various forms of non-positivism we've considered a minimal thesis that meets the explanatory demands laid out in Section 2, while preserving as much consistency as possible with a positivist framework? The question is worth exploring precisely because, as I've noted repeatedly, legal positivism is an attractively straightforward theory of law, and we should avoid taking on commitments that are more demanding than the desiderata warrant.

Here's how I propose to proceed. First, I'll observe that the most plausible explanation of why law – qua system of rules – is a goodness-fixing kind entails a qualified version of the weak natural law thesis. Next, I'll argue that our explanation of law as a goodness-fixing kind incorporates some of Hart's insights about the criteria of legality and also indirectly strengthens a dual character account of the concept of law as applied to specific rules of law. Finally, to explain the various aspects of legal practice we outlined in Section 2, including the role of moral principles in adjudication and theoretical disagreement, we'll need two supplemental assumptions: (1) that the social and moral senses of "law" jointly inform the criteria of legality as on the aggregative clustering model, and (2) that the general concept of law is a template for jurisdiction-specific concepts with more fine-grained criteria of application. Fortunately, these supplemental assumptions, I'll show, can be motivated based on our background framework for understanding goodness-fixing kinds.

3.4.1 Law as a Normative Artifact

Let us work backwards from our conclusions at the end of Section 2. As I argued there, it is exceedingly plausible that law is an abstract artifact, and, moreover, that if the Rule of Law – the kind-relative standard for evaluating laws – is to be adequately explained, then the function of law must be the realization of some very general yet limited normative ideal. This result captures, I think, the kernel of truth in the weak natural law thesis – namely, that an essentially normative criterion for evaluating law is, simultaneously, a *kind-relative* criterion of evaluation. Put differently, some defects of law characterized in essentially normative terms – its arbitrariness or unreasonableness, say – amount to *legal* defects; they make the law defective *as law*. We have left the relevant normative ideal, that is, the aspect of goodness or reasonableness at issue, underspecified, but I'll say more about its content shortly. For now, notice that what we might call the "Normative Artifact Thesis" does not entail the stronger commitments of the natural lawyer. Natural lawyers maintain that all-things-considered moral defects – and, specifically, the ineffectiveness of law at generating full-fledged moral obligations – make the law defective as law. But no such claim follows from the limited conclusions we reached at the end of Section 2.

The Normative Artifact Thesis does entail a form of non-positivism, however. Recall that there are excellent reasons for embracing the threshold condition on the existence and persistence of functional artifacts: genuine instances must effectively perform, to some degree, the artifact's constitutive function (or functions). And so, whether a social order counts as a legal system plausibly depends on its ability to minimally satisfy a normative ideal the realization of which is, ex hypothesi, law's essential function. Put differently, the existence of law is grounded in, and partly explained by, the existence of rules of social organization that are to some extent, and in a restricted sense, *good*.

On its own, the Normative Artifact Thesis is not a complete theory of law for the same reason that the strong and weak natural law theses aren't. A comprehensive theory of law should have something to say not just about the nature of law construed as a kind of social order, but also about the general criteria of legality that jurists use to discover specific *laws*. After all, we employ the concept of law to refer to systems of rules as well as specific rules of law, and presumably there is some connection across these different uses of the category. And so, it's not enough to know that the existence of a legal order depends on both social and normative conditions; we want to know how the social and normative features of rules relate to determine a rule's legality within a bona fide legal system.

3.4.2 From Normative Artifacts to Dual Character Concepts

Fortunately, an account of the "criteria of legality" can be developed in several steps. First, we leverage our explanation for the Normative Artifact Thesis – specifically, the fact that the thesis is very much embedded in, and draws inspiration from, positivist accounts of law. Recall that our earlier explanation of why law must have a normative aim relied on an independently defensible thesis proposed by positivists – namely, that law is, essentially, a system of norms that reflects higher-order structure and that's socially embraced on the basis of some normative assumptions. The idea that the social activities that produce and sustain law involve normative assumptions about law resonates, for instance, with Hart's claims about the internal point of view, Raz's claims about law's claim to authority, and Shapiro's claim that law, through its officials, has a moral aim. It is consistent, also, with the fact that legal systems throughout history have offered some justifying narrative for their existence. Such "characterizing intentions" of law-producing agents are the basis for attributing to law an essentially normative function that defines a kind-relative standard for evaluating laws. So, it wouldn't be ad hoc to borrow from positivists like Hart their account of the criteria of legality, albeit subject to a normative condition. Legal rules are rules that are validated by a jurisdiction's socially embraced rule of recognition, though the existence of a legal order, and, relatedly, the effectiveness of its rule of recognition at generating law, depends to some minimal degree on the order's normative merits.

However, we cannot rely exclusively on a Hartian view of the criteria of legality, even supplemented by a normative threshold condition, for the reasons Dworkin gave. No such criteria satisfactorily explain, whether in vindicating or debunking terms, such features of legal reasoning as the treatment of moral principles as a source of law. Moreover, throughout legal history, jurists have felt free to invoke principles of impartiality, reciprocity, and the like as law and on seemingly a priori grounds, when their entitlement to do so rarely seems secure on the basis of the jurisdiction's rule of recognition alone. Indeed, such practices have persisted in jurisdictions with persistent disagreement about the grounds of law, and disagreement, specifically, about whether the moral content of a principle, on its own, suffices for its legality. So, the Hartian view couldn't be complete.

Fortunately, the considerations that justify the Normative Artifact Thesis also suggest a principled and explanatorily powerful supplementation of Hart's account of the criteria. Once we've acknowledged law's essentially normative function, together with the fact that this function arises in the standard way for artifactual kinds (i.e., through the psychology of creators and sustainers), we've indirectly strengthened the case for something like a dual character account of the *concept* of law, at least in its application to individual rules within a legal system. Recall that the dual character account maintains that there are distinct but related criteria of application for the legal concept. And dual character accounts were originally motivated based on artifactual concepts, especially artifacts with ostensibly normative functions, such as artworks, including plays, paintings, symphonies, and novels (Lio et al. 2020). Plausibly, the function of artworks is to be valuable in some restricted sense, given the intentions of those involved in their production (the conceivers, creators, and sustainers). And relatedly, there appear to be both social and normative senses of "art," at least when the concept is used to pick out specific instances. We sometimes recognize objects as art simply for being housed in a museum or in virtue of being judged as art by a community of artists, thus applying purely social criteria of classification tied to art's production and recognition. But it is also entirely common to employ normative criteria based on what is plausibly art's evaluative function. One can coherently and without conceptual confusion refrain from calling something art, despite its social recognition as such, that isn't appropriately moving, interesting, or otherwise *aesthetically valuable*.[78] Moreover, there is evidence in the

---

[78] When employed this way, the concept ART is an essentially normative concept. To call something art is to endorse it based on a broad set of aesthetic values and virtues. For an illuminating discussion of the way both "practice-internal" and "practice-external" reasons, values, and

historical record of the application of art-concepts exclusively in terms of normative and abstract (as opposed to social) criteria, even ostensibly a priori classifications of natural phenomena entirely uninfluenced by human agency as "natural artworks."[79] Given the similarities in conceptual practices, one would expect the concept of law, when applied to specific rules of law, to similarly involve social and normative criteria, where the latter tracks a rule's contribution to the realization of the normative ideal that constitutes law's function.

The dual character account thus pairs well with the Normative Artifact Thesis insofar as the thesis' justification, together with general facts about dual character concepts, explains why legal expressions might have dual senses (so we don't just have to accept the dual character account on abductive grounds: as a hypothesis that explains the linguistic data highlighted by its proponents). However, we still need to know how the social and the normative criteria of application relate. For reasons discussed earlier, law's essential function, though essentially normative, cannot be the realization of some overly specific moral ideal, for the resulting view would impute implausible intentions to agents involved in the production of legal orders. So, it's not yet obvious why specific moral principles have been regarded as law on seemingly conceptual grounds.

3.4.3 On Concept[s] of Law: The Clustering and Fine-graining of the Criteria of Legality

One possibility is that the relationship between the social and normative criteria is captured by the model of an aggregative cluster concept. The criterion of legality is, always, some weighted combination of two factors: (1) how close a rule is, given its content, to being derivable from (or entailed by) the socially embraced rule of recognition, and (2) how it contributes to the law's realization of its normative aspirations. We needn't assume, as Dworkin did, that there must be some single "best" way of balancing considerations of "fit" and "justification."

---

norms inform our aesthetic judgments, see Kubala (2021). On "art concept pluralism" and the distinction between "conventional art" and "aesthetic art," see, e.g., Mag Uidhir and Magnus (2011: pp. 90–92). For a related distinction in legal theory, between internal and external statements of law, see Toh (2011).

[79] See Clark and Rehding's (2006) discussion of the traditional view of music as "a fact of external nature" – as sound-structures discovered by the musician – in contrast to the view of "music as the interior moral power of human nature." As in the legal case, one needn't endorse such contested claims within the practice of art to appreciate the flexibility of the operative concepts. The relevant fact to be explained is simply that the historical record is full of references to so-called natural artworks and nature's artistic prowess. Such claims plausibly involve the application of art-concepts based exclusively on the values or ideals that art is meant to realize rather than social or agential criteria. For a theory of musical artifacts based on the model of discovery, selection, and indication by the artist (rather than literal creation), see Levinson (1980). For a defense of the assumption that all art is the product of a successful "art-intention," see Mag Uidhir (2013).

Any such strong assumption would have to be motivated. But the weaker assumption that, in general, the social and normative properties of rules *together* inform legal classification has an explanatory payoff. Recall that positivist explanations of the legality of moral principles weren't altogether unreasonable. The social conditions concerning, for example, what's customary within legal systems may not have fit the legality of moral principles perfectly given disagreement among jurists. But there has always been some degree of recognition, among significant groups of jurists, of the a priori legality of moral principles. The moral features of such principles may have compensated for their imperfect fit with more broadly shared customs and tradition. I say "may" and have hedged my claims here in an effort to remain neutral on the intra-systemic question of legal substance: whether judges were *right* to classify the relevant principles (or, on the opposite extreme, socially embraced yet utterly wicked principles) as law. The goal is to charitably explain judicial behavior as neither bizarre nor dishonest, not to establish that some claim made by this or that judge is correct (or incorrect). The correctness of the relevant claims is dialectically contested and not a pretheoretical datum. Accordingly, our explanation should be neither plainly vindicating nor debunking; it should be *rationalizing*.

Still, it's unclear how much progress has been made towards rationalizing legal behavior. If the normative criteria of legality are very general and limited (as we've assumed they must be if they derive from law's essential function), then the criteria presumably validate many different principles that are socially embraced to varying degrees. They wouldn't necessarily pick out, say, the principle the court in *Riggs* relied on, which invalidated a claim to inheritance on grounds of injustice to the decedent. For a contrary principle, enforcing the claim in the absence of express statutory prohibition, might have been equally consistent with the formal Rule of Law and the limited normative ideal it captures. Indeed, the dissenting justice emphasized as much – that enforcing the will as written would be *in a sense* fair, especially given that the criminal law would punish the injustice at issue.[80]

We can solve this problem by leveraging yet another general and entirely familiar feature of artifactual kinds. Once we acquire concepts of such kinds (the concept of a knife, say), we easily grasp more fine-grained or precisified concepts (carving knife, paring knife, utility knife, army knife, and so on). These more fine-grained concepts involve further specification of the social/agential and functional properties that define the general category.[81] So, it's

---

[80] 22 NE 188, 191-2 (NY 1889).
[81] What follows is best understood as a hypothesis about how to model conceptual combination in the case of complex artifact-concepts, a hypothesis supported by its usefulness in explaining categorization and reasoning.

plausible that the more specific normative criteria jurists have sometimes relied on in deeming, on seemingly a priori grounds, specific moral principles as law derive not from the concept of law *as such* (although some limited normative principles may well derive from the general concept), but from more fine-grained concepts of *American law, Roman law,* and other kinds of law. Far from being ad hoc, the assumption is a natural one to make given the broader theory of artifacts we're relying on. Concepts of American law or Roman law don't just involve more specific social properties (being a legal order embraced by Americans) than the general concept but also more specific normative properties (for instance, as the US constitution indicates, the property of being a system of rules that is not just good in terms of Rule-of-Law fairness but conducive to "the general welfare, and ... the blessings of liberty to ourselves and our Posterity").[82] Concepts of normative or value-driven artifacts exhibit precisely this structure. The criteria for being a classical, romantic, or impressionist art song, involve further specification of the non-normative as well as normative criteria for being an art song. Whereas an art song must instantiate to some extent some very general aesthetic ideal, romantic art songs plausibly exhibit a specific form of aesthetic goodness – a distinctively romantic aesthetic. Likewise, the criteria for being an expressionist painting or an abstract painting or a renaissance painting, and so on, are plausibly specifications of the more general non-normative and normative criteria for being a painting. Notice, also, that it's more plausible to ascribe relatively specific moralistic intentions to Americans involved in the creation and sustaining of *American law* than it would be to attribute such intentions to every community that has ever created or sustained a legal order. The normative intentions that are shared across legal systems must be very general and indeterminate; but they can be more specific in the case of individual legal systems.

The resulting explanation of the role of moral principles in legal reasoning might seem superficially similar to the explanation offered by "inclusive positivists" (see Section 2.2). But there are important differences, and the comparison will prove helpful for further clarifying the present view and its ability to better explain judicial practice. Inclusive positivists allow that moral principles could enjoy the status of legality within a legal system, but they insist that what makes such principles *law* are contingent social facts within the system – specifically, facts that ground the system's more fundamental or higher-order

---

[82] Obviously, that's not to say that there are as many fine-grained concepts of law as there are individual states or jurisdictions. As I discuss later, we should only posit more fine-grained concepts when necessary to explain the conceptual practices of distinct legal-linguistic communities, and specifically based on the kinds of legal claims that participants find primitively compelling.

laws, whose legality is a function of social conditions alone.[83] Put differently, the inclusive positivist thinks that there is a jurisdiction-relative truth of the form "there is a rule of law (around here) that entails that moral principle x is law," a truth that is ultimately grounded in some degree of behavioral convergence among officials in the system.[84] So, for example, American officials might embrace a rule of recognition that treats moral principles as law in cases like *Riggs*. Recall from our earlier discussion that this style of explanation seemed strained upon examination. The problem is that there is nothing resembling socio-legal consensus within the relevant jurisdictions on the legal classification of moral principles. The *Riggs* dissent emphasized as much by questioning whether American courts can or should behave as the majority did. On top of that, judges who treat moral principles as law seem to be relying on a priori (and moral) intuition, and not just sizing up social consensus in arriving at their rulings.

On the present view, judges who find primitively compelling a proposition of the form "moral principle x is law$_{\text{American}}$" are simply relying on a conception of AMERICAN LAW on which the proposition is a basic conceptual truth sustained by the concept's criteria of application being essentially moral. Our concepts are often revealed in the propositions we find primitively compelling (think *all bachelors are unmarried*). A proposition is *primitively* compelling if it is compelling but not in virtue of other propositions/inferences one finds compelling (cf. Peacocke 1992; Davis 2005; Rabin 2020). That judges our disposed to find the relevant legal propositions primitively compelling should no longer seem mysterious now that we've subsumed the disposition under a more general and familiar one reflected in our conceptual practices involving normative or value-driven artifacts. As previously discussed, concepts with essentially normative criteria of application are easily acquired based on our interactions with artifacts with normative functions, such as artworks. It's a separate question, however, whether and to what degree such essentially normative concepts are widely shared. For example, if the concept AMERICAN LAW as understood by the *Riggs* court is widely shared, that would amount to a kind of social fact, but one that is very different from the social facts that ground rules of law and that the *Riggs* court needn't have had access to for its approach to be rationalizable. Let us unpack these points slowly. On a plausible account of concept possession, agents possess a concept in virtue of finding certain truths (or truth-preserving inferences) involving the concept primitively compelling in idealized

---

[83] See discussion in 2.2.
[84] Positivists disagree about how much convergence is required to ground a higher-order rule of law, but they agree that convergence is based on the actual observable behavior of relevant officials. See Hart (1994: pp. 95, 102), Raz (1979: pp. 95–96), Leiter (1995), and Kramer (2018: p. 84).

circumstances (for example, with full information about the facts relevant to its application). This entails that the concept AMERICAN LAW might be shared despite plenty of *actual* disagreement over whether some candidate moral principle (e.g., the *Riggs* principle of not letting persons profit from their own wrongdoing) qualifies as law. Naturally, judges don't have access to facts concerning what their linguistic community *would* find primitively compelling in circumstances of full information (about social, moral, linguistic, and other facts). A judge's assumption that her understanding of the concept will attract convergence in ideal circumstances (and so qualify as "shared") may be based on nothing more than a hunch, intuitive seeming, or leap of faith. But that's not a unique feature of the legal case; it is a general phenomenon: our intuitions about sharing a concept with others (1) are often "epistemically primitive," (2) withstand conflicting conceptual starting points or basic intuitions within the community, and (3) tend not to be based on a systematic survey of past usage and present dispositions to apply associated terminology in actual and counterfactual scenarios (see, e.g., Schroeter 2012: pp. 191–192).[85]

Of course, how we come to have the basic conceptual dispositions that we do and why our intuitions about concept-sharing are often reliable turn on complex issues in the philosophy of language.[86] My strategy in this section has been to locate the basic dispositions we find among jurists within our broader conceptual practices involving normative artifacts. But we needn't resolve, here, the nature of concepts, concept possession, or concept mastery to recognize the basic point that the rules that govern our concepts, and that may or may not be shared by others, are very different from rules of *law*, and relatedly, that our present explanation of judicial practice diverges substantially from the inclusive positivist's explanation, and in ways that make it better as an explanation. Among other things, rules of law are embraced with a greater degree of self-consciousness (recall the importance of Hart's "internal point of view") and by a select few in the linguistic community designated as "officials."[87] Moreover, as positivists often remind us, not all rules that jurists rely on in adjudication count as *legal* rules just for being relied on. Our conceptual dispositions in relation to normative artifacts together with general norms of communication – in particular, the fact that our basic conceptual commitments needn't be based

---

[85] Schroeter (2012) suggests that the reliability of these primitive appearances of "samesaying" might be based on a willingness to adjust one's own conception based on the fully informed understandings and intuitions of others. Since we don't take ourselves to be using arbitrary stipulative categories, our private representational practices are rarely decisive.

[86] The literature on concept individuation, possession, and mastery is complex. I point the interested reader to the work of Lewis (1975), Burge (1979), Peacocke (1992), Brandom (1994), Horwich (2005), Davis (2005), and Schroeter (2012). Rabin (2018) provides a helpful overview of some important themes.

[87] See, e.g., Leiter (2021), who describes the rule of recognition as a rule that officials "treat as obligatory" given their actual practice.

on convergent behavior within our linguistic community – enable the present view to explain: (a) why judges classify morally good principles as law on purely conceptual, moral, and a priori grounds; (b) why they do so despite lack of convergence among jurists; and even (c) why they might ultimately be vindicated. Their dissenting peers may find the classifications primitively compelling in idealized circumstances (e.g., in circumstances of moral enlightenment).[88] There are other important differences between inclusive positivism and the view I've outlined, concerning, for instance, whether the legality of some thin normative principles is entailed by the general jurisdiction-independent concept of law.[89]

We thus have the contours of a rationalizing explanation for the role of specific moral principles in legal reasoning, albeit an explanation whose details might vary by jurisdiction. Can this emerging theory of law also explain persistent theoretical disagreement? It can certainly leverage persistent moral disagreements in explanation. Since people disagree about what justice, virtue, and the good require, they will, presumably, also disagree about which precise features of rules determine their legality, even if they share a concept of law with partly moral criteria of application. Moreover, our theory offers additional explanatory resources when theoretical disagreements about law aren't rooted in moral disagreements. We've assumed that the concept of law involves an imprecise aggregation of broadly social and moral properties of rules. As discussed earlier, aggregative cluster concepts are often indeterminate. Competent use of such concepts involves understanding a range of "easy" or prototypical applications (cf. Finnis 1980). In the case of law, the straightforward extension includes rules that are largely consistent with jurisdiction-specific social practice and, simultaneously, morally acceptable to some degree.

---

[88] Notice that this account leaves room for the *Riggs* majority and the dissent to be engaged in a good faith disagreement about a shared subject matter, AMERICAN LAW, despite their inconsistent conceptions of that subject in nonideal circumstances. Moreover, by leaving open the possibility of a good faith disagreement between jurists, our account avoids having to (a) speculate about their "true" motivations or (b) paraphrase their claims. Contrast, for instance, an interpretation of bedrock juridical disagreements as a "meta-linguistic negotiation"; see Plunkett and Sundell (2013b) and the discussion in 1.3.

[89] Recall from our earlier discussion in 2.2 that inclusive positivists maintain that there are *no* moral or essentially normative principles whose legality can be secured on conceptual grounds alone and independently of jurisdiction-specific social facts. On the present view, at least some thin normative ideals are *legal* ideals in all jurisdictions, whose legality is derived from the general concept of law as a value-driven artifact. The ideal of the Rule of Law constrains the very existence of a legal system. Inclusive positivists have traditionally denied that the normative characteristics of a legal system bear on its existence. Finally, the moderate strain of non-positivism I've defended in this section consists of more than just an account of the criteria of legal validity, and my overall argument for the view differs substantially from the case Waluchow (1994), Coleman (2001), Kramer (2004), and others have made for inclusive positivism.

Dworkin was thus correct in thinking that all it takes to be a competent user of the concept of law – to *possess* the concept as opposed to mastering it – is to know the core of the institutional practices to be interpreted. However, competent use of the concept does *not* require applying some precise aggregation principle that would decide hard cases – that is, cases involving rules whose social and moral properties diverge radically in their legal implications.

Nevertheless, jurists may end up endorsing competing claims about the grounds of (American, English, Roman ...) law that are more precise (or fine-grained) than is conceptually warranted for a range of understandable reasons. Indeterminacy in the concept(s) of law needn't be obvious.[90] And so long as a candidate precisification of the concept is compatible with the core of legal practice, it might seem plausible as an account of the concept's criteria of application, especially if enough others in the relevant linguistic community endorse the precisification. It is, thus, possible that participants in theoretical legal disagreements have competing beliefs about the precise criteria of application that ideal reasoners in the jurisdiction – those who reason correctly about social, moral, linguistic, and perhaps even philosophical matters – will converge on. This final step in the argument is admittedly speculative, but no more so, I submit, than any other explanation of persistent theoretical disagreement in the literature, a phenomenon that may well amount to one of the more challenging puzzles in legal philosophy. Nevertheless, I hope I've demonstrated that the view we've developed has several resources for explaining it.

***

We've covered a lot of ground in this final section and so a summary might be helpful. My primary goal throughout has been to clearly state a pared-down non-positivist hypothesis about law and ask – both positivists and non-positivists – why it couldn't be true. If the view suffers from some obvious flaw, presumably it will come to light when its core commitments are summarized, and so here they are.

---

[90] Indeterminacy certainly doesn't follow from the mere fact that officials in a legal system don't agree on a precise rule of recognition. Indeed, while it's quite obvious that socially embraced higher-order rules of interpretation and adjudication in, say, the American legal system won't settle the originalism/nonoriginalism debate (since there is no actual consensus among legal officials), it is far less obvious whether the concept AMERICAN LAW is similarly indeterminate with respect to the debate. For reasons I've noted, whether and in what ways the concept is indeterminate turns on more complex considerations than just the actual behavior and commitments of legal officials. It might turn, for instance, on their dispositions to employ legal language in idealized circumstances of full (social, moral, linguistic ...) information. Since we don't have direct access to such dispositions, the best we can do is formulate a hypothesis about the shared concept that is then tested for explanatory and theoretical adequacy. Indeed, I've argued for conceptual indeterminacy based primarily on considerations of explanatory power and fit with a broader conceptual scheme and not the mere fact of actual disagreement.

Law, construed as a system of rules, is, fundamentally, a kind of abstract artifact: a system of rules conceived, adopted, and sustained through purposive agential activity. Like other such artifactual kinds, law has an essential or constitutive function: the realization of a normative ideal. I haven't had much to say about the ingredients of this normative ideal, which may be somewhat disappointing, though, as I indicated earlier, a promising account might be found in Railton's (2019) discussion of the ideal of the Rule of Law. Cataloging the ideal as precisely as we can seems to me to be a project for moral psychologists, or psychologists of legal moralism.[91]

Nevertheless, we have, I think, successfully motivated certain constraints on this ideal. It captures only some of the reasons that bear on action. We can call them "moral" reasons solely to emphasize that the reasons are genuine, deliberatively relevant, and objectively worth attending to. But that doesn't mean that the law's constitutive "goodness" entails all-things-considered moral obligations to follow the law. Recall that we want to avoid the problems for traditional non-positivism posed by immoral laws as well as mundane and morally neutral laws that are legally obligatory but not morally so (see Section 3.2). Nevertheless, the normative characterization of law by legal actors tracks an objective normative property, sensitivity to which may be connected to living in and striving to protect a cooperative legal order or civil society.

Given general principles governing artifactual kinds, the existence and persistence of law – that is, a *legal* order – is grounded, partly, in the social acceptance of rules with certain formal characteristics (roughly those described by HLA Hart), and, partly, in the minimal conformity of the system to the normative ideal whose realization is law's constitutive function. When a legal system realizes to some extent the relevant ideal, the fact that it does is an essentially normative fact. And so, a normative fact, concerning how *good* a legal system is, in some selective and underspecified sense, partly grounds its being a *legal* system.

Furthermore, we employ the concept of law to refer not just to systems of rules but to specific rules of law within legal systems. The concepts associated with other normative or value-driven artifacts function similarly. And when the legal concept is used in this way, the criteria of application exhibit dual character structure and aggregative multi-dimensionality: in determining whether

---

[91] However, we shouldn't expect a non-normative specification of the ideal to fully capture its normativity. When a legal system realizes the ideal, the fact that it does is an essentially normative fact. Admittedly, I'm relying here on my own meta-normative commitments – specifically, skepticism about reductive accounts of normativity. On the relevance of meta-normative theory generally, see Section 4.

a rule falls under the concept, users of legal language rely on both social criteria, such as the rule's similarity to one derivable from a socially embraced rule of recognition, as well as normative criteria, such as the rule's contribution to law's normative aspirations. Both properties count in favor of the rule's legality, but the contribution each property makes (and what, in aggregate, counts as legal sufficiency) is indeterminate. Conceptual competence follows from an understanding of easy and prototypical cases of law, where the social and normative properties of rules more or less point in the same direction. Hard cases involving divergence inspire understandable disagreement, even understandable errors within a community based on the assumption that the concept of law affords greater precision. Finally, the general concept of law lends itself to further specification, with system-specific concepts of AMERICAN LAW or ROMAN LAW, defined in terms of more fine-grained social and normative criteria of application. Moral properties of rules may have greater legal significance in some such jurisdictions on conceptual grounds alone, and not because a fundamental law within the system, such as a legal rule of recognition, confers the status of legality on moral principles.

The resulting view amounts to a moderate strain of legal non-positivism, one that locates law within a broader conceptual framework involving artifactual, functional, and goodness-fixing kinds. Its core commitments have been motivated based on clearly defined desiderata and general features of the broader explanatory scheme on which it relies. The theory explains why law is susceptible to kind-relative evaluation and why certain characteristics of law are widely recognized as law's constitutive virtues, without departing from general theories of functional and goodness-fixing kinds. It explains, with considerable neutrality on questions of legal substance and without undermotivated lack of charity towards legal actors, the contested classification of moral principles as a form of a priori law, juridical reliance on moral principles in adjudication, and persistent theoretical disagreement about the grounds of law. The explanation leverages general truths about our conceptual practices involving artifacts with normative functions. The overall view has these virtues without insisting on a counterintuitive correspondence between legal and moral facts, or on a robust obligation to follow the law wherever there is law, or on law's moral defects being essentially legal defects. I don't mean to suggest that that the view I've sketched has no theoretical costs in comparison to, say, Hartian positivism. In fact, I'll address shortly what seems to me to be the most salient cost (shared with other forms of non-positivism): namely, that the account makes liberal use of normative concepts as well as an ontology of normative properties and facts. Additionally, the account is clearly more baroque than Hart's view, but a view that is complex in principled ways doesn't have to be "frilly." That is, it needn't take on undermotivated commitments that make legal non-positivism a more difficult position to defend than it needs to be. This should advance the theory's prospects of wider acceptance.

4 Outstanding Questions

We have considered objections to specific versions of non-positivism as they have come up. But questions remain that arise regardless of the form a non-positivist view takes, including the relatively moderate position I outlined at the end of the previous section. In what follows, I offer a brief discussion of two important challenges confronting the non-positivist research program. The discussion is brief because addressing these challenges comprehensively would take us too far afield and the present goal is limited to identifying lines of further inquiry.

4.1 Meta-normative Anxieties

The overall case for non-positivism has the structure of an inference to the best explanation. We identified some facts about laws and legal systems that would be hard to explain if positivism were true. And so, we explored non-positivist theories that promise to explain everything that positivists can explain and more. But introducing new theoretical machinery can be costly insofar as it generates new explanatory burdens. The case for non-positivism only succeeds if the explanatory gains over positivism aren't outweighed by the costs. And one salient cost, or at least an aspect of the non-positivist paradigm that makes some theorists nervous, is its unqualified embrace of a vocabulary and ontology of the good and the right.

Here's one way of fleshing out the concern. Legal non-positivists maintain that the existence of a legal system depends on a system of rules being, as a matter of fact, *good* in some moral or robustly normative sense. That makes the existence of a legal system seem to depend on uncertain matters, for one might have doubts about whether *anything* could be good "as a matter fact." There is certainly no consensus among philosophers about what our normative thought and talk commits us to, and whether our commitments – including assumptions about the factuality of moral discourse – are ultimately justified (see, e.g., van Roojen 2023). By contrast, the existence of legal systems doesn't seem all that uncertain or controversial, which seems like a problem for non-positivists. And there may be other ways in which meta-normative uncertainty puts pressure on the view.[92]

---

[92] Consider persistent disagreements about the content of the good and the right. Maybe such disagreements undercut the plausibility of the claim (endorsed by positivists and non-positivists

I suspect such concerns to be the main source of resistance to non-positivism, despite positivism's explanatory gaps. If that's right, then reinvigorating the non-positivist research program crucially depends on explaining why we get to be relaxed about our meta-normative commitments. Unfortunately, reasons of space prevent me from doing justice to this important issue, which also happens to be underdiscussed in the broader literature. Nevertheless, we should be able to articulate in broad strokes the case for evaluating non-positivism independently of our meta-normative anxieties. For the view is compatible with *any* viable position one might hold in meta-normative theory, at least in principle.

To begin with, although it might seem like non-positivists must assume the existence of objective normative facts, this turns out not to be true. The crucial point of non-positivism is that our legal categories take some broadly objectivist assumptions about morality and normativity for granted – that is, in classifying social orders as *law*, we take for granted that the relevant orders *in fact* exhibit certain normative features, like reasonableness or authority. Non-positivists endorse this claim because we think it best explains legal reasoning and practice. But the normative assumptions essentially involved in legal classification could very well turn out to be false and for reasons entirely unrelated to law (more below) without undercutting the truth of non-positivism.[93] And so, non-positivism should be evaluated based exclusively on whether it offers the best explanation of legal reasoning and practice. It shouldn't be saddled with a further theoretical obligation to "vindicate" objectivist ethics.

To ground the point by way of example, suppose a meta-normative "error theory" turns out to be true (see, e.g., Mackie 1977). The error theorist thinks that there are strictly speaking no facts of goodness or rightness, whether concerning law or anything else. Our normative judgments attribute properties to acts, situations, and states of affairs that they in fact lack. If both a meta-normative error theory and non-positivism turn out to be true, it would entail that some of the assumptions we make when we describe specific rules (or bodies of rules) as law are mistaken – specifically, the assumptions concerning law's goodness. Non-positivism would thus turn out to be a qualified error theory about law. But this wouldn't entail anything so absurd as the nonexistence of rules and social orders that we have in mind and intend to refer to using our legal expressions. For even defective concepts can serve our communicative ends of referring *de re* to, or focusing conversational attention on, genuine

---

alike) that some normative assumptions about law – its reasonableness or authority, say – are widely shared among officials involved in the production and sustaining of legal orders.

[93] Indeed, some versions of non-positivism, such as the dual character theory, seem to me to be agnostic on whether laws in fact exhibit the moral properties our concepts ascribe to them.

things in the world that our concepts misdescribe.[94] Legal non-positivism is thus compatible with a meta-normative error theory, although I'm not sure I know anyone who explicitly endorses this position.

That said, given that defenders of non-positivism usually embrace more optimistic meta-normative commitments (see, e.g., Finnis 2011; Dworkin 2011: pp. 23–94; Greenberg 2008), it would be good to say something in defense of the view in its standard packaging. And the main point to note in this regard is that there is a plausible research program in contemporary metaethics that's committed to showing not just that the error theory is false but that a commitment to normative facts and, more generally, to the objectivity of moral reasoning does *not* involve taking on any dubious metaphysical commitments. For instance, metaethical "quasi-realists" maintain that moral judgments have a practical function of expressing the speaker's practical attitudes – for instance, their support for or aversion to specific actions, rules, or states of affairs – but that this attitude-expressive function is perfectly compatible with the existence of moral facts, the objectivity of moral reasoning, and a naturalistic worldview (see, e.g., Blackburn 1984, Gibbard 2003).[95] I cannot elaborate on the justifications for quasi-realism here. The point I'm making is just that if such relaxed forms of moral ("quasi-")realism can be absorbed "off the shelf" by non-positivism, then non-positivists don't necessarily incur any unique costs in terms of their metaphysical commitments as compared to positivists.

Finally, even if it turns out that the best version of legal non-positivism requires embracing a more controversial version of moral realism committed, say, to a "non-natural" realm of irreducibly moral facts and properties (see, e.g., Enoch 2011), that wouldn't, on its own, count in favor of positivism. I don't deny that in this scenario, non-positivists would bear a unique justificatory burden, since whether there are any such facts and properties is entirely nonobvious. My point is just that insofar as the viability of robust moral realism is philosophically contested, the truth or falsity of the view will invariably be a point of contestation within the philosophy of law as well.

---

[94] For a general discussion of why an error theory about a domain of discourse needn't undercut the usefulness or practical point of the discourse, see Burgess (1998).

[95] Traditionally, quasi-realists like Blackburn and Gibbard have endeavored to vindicate objectivist claims in metaethics based on minimalist accounts of the concept of truth and related idioms of objectivity. See discussion in Salinger (2023). For an alternative approach to the objectivity of our moral commitments that is, in principle, compatible with quasi-realism, see Atiq (2021: pp. 14052–14056). For an application of expressivist accounts of normative judgment (but not quasi-realism) to legal theory, see Toh (2011).

4.2 The Stakes

Let's assume that a relaxed moral realism can be made to work and turn to a different challenge that's best evaluated at the end of our discussion. Even if some form of non-positivism turns out to be true, we haven't yet ruled out the possibility that it would be a *better* world, as in morally or practically better, if we reoriented our social practices around a category that fits the basic elements of a positivist characterization, call it "law$_P$."[96] As I noted at the outset, I won't be making a practical case for non-positivism, and so the question of whether non-positivist assumptions and practices lead to better outcomes (for, say, litigants and other legal subjects) remains unanswered. Yet the practical question is a natural one to raise having examined the nature of our existing practices. Once we've understood a salient and consequential aspect of our social world, it's sensible to ask how and whether it can be improved. Indeed, our work has clarified what it would take to successfully reorient our thinking and behavior around laws$_P$ and legal$_P$ systems, and what we would be giving up. Legal$_P$ practice would reflect very different assumptions about moral principles (whether and when it's appropriate for judges to rely on them), the rule of law (i.e., the criteria for distinctly legal evaluation), theoretical disagreements (their very possibility), and the history of legal systems (whether and to what extent past legal systems are continuous with our current practices). Any serious reformist would have to face up to the question of whether it's even possible to extricate the non-positivist assumptions that regulate legal reasoning and behavior.

But even if it turns out that there are good and actionable reasons to revise our practices, our efforts would not have been for naught. For quite apart from needing a philosophy of law to help us understand the world as we find it, there is an intellectual payoff that transcends our legal categories. Law turns out to be embedded in a broader conceptual scheme that is worth understanding in its own right, and that is, in turn, better understood when its interaction with law is clarified. To illustrate, the moderate strain of non-positivism I've defended is very much motivated based on a precise understanding of artifactual, functional, and goodness-fixing kinds, not to mention the language we use to conceptualize and refer to such kinds. It should be no surprise, then, that the value of the philosophical enterprise tends to be most apparent to those immersed in it and may elude those who haven't followed the argument. It takes systematic reflection to appreciate that our reasoning about laws and legal

---

[96] In Section 1.3, I identified several authors who make a practical case for positivism. On "reformist" projects generally and the possibility of "conceptual ethics," see McPherson and Plunkett (2024).

systems is richly complex, and that through the study of law in full generality, we come to have a better grasp on the nature of value-driven artifacts, functions, group agency, morality, kind-relative evaluation, and interpretation. What would thus be effective as a critique of our descriptive (rather than practical) methodology is a demonstration that despite our efforts to be systemic, we ended up overlooking general features of laws and legal systems that invite explanation. And the right response to such a critique would be an even more systematic philosophy of law.

References

Alexy, R. (2010a). *The argument from injustice: A reply to legal positivism* (1st paperback ed.). New York: Oxford University Press.

Alexy, R. (2010b). The dual nature of law. *Ratio Juris*, 23(2): 167–182.

Alexy, R. (2021). *Law's ideal dimension*. Oxford: Oxford University Press.

Almeida, G. (2023). A dual character theory of law. *Journal of Legal Philosophy*, 49: 1–24. https://doi.org/10.2139/ssrn.4065049.

Atiq, E. H. (2019). Legal obligation & its limits. *Law and Philosophy*, 38(2): 109–147.

Atiq, E. H. (2020a). There are no easy counterexamples to legal anti-positivism. *Journal of Ethics and Social Philosophy*, 17(1): 1–26. https://doi.org/10.26556/jesp.v17i1.701.

Atiq, E. H. (2020b). Review of natural law and the nature of law. *Notre Dame Philosophical Reviews*. https://ndpr.nd.edu/reviews/natural-law-and-the-nature-of-law/.

Atiq, E. H. (2021). Acquaintance, knowledge, and value. *Synthese*, 199(5–6): 14035–14062. https://doi.org/10.1007/s11229-021-03409-9.

Atiq, E. H. (2023). Legal positivism and the moral origins of legal systems. *Canadian Journal of Law & Jurisprudence*, 36(1): 37–64. https://doi.org/10.1017/cjlj.2022.17.

Atiq, E. H. (forthcoming, 2025). Law, the rule of law, and goodness-fixing kinds. In K. Brownlee, D. Enoch, & A. Marmor (eds.), *Engaging Raz: Themes in normative philosophy*. Oxford University Press. https://philpapers.org/rec/ATILTR.

Atiq, E. H., & Mathews, J. (2022). The uncertain foundations of public law theory. *Cornell Journal of Law & Public Policy*, 31: 389–450.

Austin, J. (1832) [1995]. *The province of jurisprudence determined*, W. E. Rumble (ed.). Cambridge: Cambridge University Press. https://doi.org/10.1017/CBO9780511521546.

Banner, S. (2021). *The decline of natural law: How American lawyers once used natural law and why they stopped* (1st ed.). New York: Oxford University Press. https://doi.org/10.1093/oso/9780197556498.001.0001.

Barney, R. (2023). Platonic qua-predication. *Analytic Philosophy*, 65(4): 453–472.

Baude, W., & Sachs, S. (2019). Grounding originalism. *Northwestern University Law Review*, 113: 1455–1492.

Berman, M. N. (2022). Dworkin versus hart revisited: The challenge of non-lexical determination. *Oxford Journal of Legal Studies*, 42(2): 548–577.

Blackburn, S. (1984). *Spreading the word*. Oxford: Oxford University Press.

Brandom, R. (1994). *Making it explicit: Reasoning, representing, and discursive commitment*. Cambridge: Harvard University Press.

Burge, T. (1979). Individualism and the mental. *Midwest Studies in Philosophy*, IV: 73–122.

Burgess, J. A. (1998). Error theories and values. *Australasian Journal of Philosophy*, 76(4): 534–552.

Chalmers, D. J., & Jackson, F. (2001). Conceptual analysis and reductive explanation. *The Philosophical Review*, 110(3): 315–360. https://doi.org/10.1215/00318108-110-3-315.

Chilovi, S., & Pavlakos, G. (2019). Law-determination as grounding: A common grounding framework for jurisprudence. *Legal Theory*, 25(1): 53–76.

Chilovi, S., & Pavlakos, G. (2022). The explanatory demands of grounding in law. *Pacific Philosophical Quarterly*, 103(4): 900–933.

Clark, S., & Rehding, A. (2006). *Music theory and natural order from the renaissance to the early twentieth century*. Cambridge: Cambridge University Press.

Coleman, J. L. (2001). *The practice of principle: In defense of a pragmatist approach to legal theory*. Oxford: Oxford University Press.

Corwin, E. S. (1928). The "higher law" background of American constitutional law. *Harvard Law Review*, 42(3): 365.

Crowe, J. (2019). *Natural law and the nature of law*. Cambridge: Cambridge University Press.

Cummins, R. (1975). Functional explanation. *The Journal of Philosophy*, 72: 741–764.

Dancy, J. (2004). *Ethics without principles*. New York: Oxford University Press.

Davis, W. A. (2005). Concept individuation, possession conditions, and propositional attitudes. *Noûs*, 39(1): 140–166.

Dindjer, H. (2020). The new legal anti-positivism. *Legal Theory*, 26(3): 181–213. https://doi.org/10.1017/S1352325220000208.

Donelson, R., & Hannikainen, I. R. (2020). Fuller and the folk: The inner morality of law revisited. In T. Lombrozo, J. Knobe, & S. Nichols (eds.), *Oxford studies in experimental philosophy*, vol. 3. Oxford: Oxford University Press, 6–28.

Dummett, M. (1993). *Seas of language*. Oxford: Oxford University Press.

Dworkin, R. (1967). The model of rules. *The University of Chicago Law Review*, 35(1): 14–46.

Dworkin, R. (1974). Hard cases. *Harvard Law Review*, 88: 1057.

Dworkin, R. (1986a). *A matter of principle*. Cambridge: Harvard University Press.

Dworkin, R. (1986b). *Law's Empire*. Cambridge: Harvard University Press.

Dworkin, R. (1996). *Freedom's law: The moral reading of the American constitution*. Cambridge: Harvard University Press.

Dworkin, R. (2011). *Justice for hedgehogs*. Cambridge: Harvard University Press.

Ehrenberg, K. (2016). *The functions of law*. Oxford: Oxford University Press.

Enoch, D. (2011). *Taking morality seriously*. Oxford: Oxford University Press.

Evnine, S. J. (2016). *Making objects and events: A hylomorphic theory of artifacts, actions, and organisms*. Oxford: Oxford University Press.

Ewing, B. (2017). Conventionality, disagreement, and fidelity. *Canadian Journal of Law & Jurisprudence*, 30: 97.

Fine, K. (1994). Essence and modality. *Philosophical Perspectives*, 8: 1–16.

Finnis, J. (1987). On reason and authority in law's empire. *Law and Philosophy*, 6(3): 357–380. https://doi.org/10.1007/BF00142932.

Finnis, J. (2007). Grounds of law and legal theory: A response. *Legal Theory*, 13 (3–4): 315–344. https://doi.org/10.1017/S1352325208070122.

Finnis, J. (2011). *Natural law and natural rights* (2nd ed.). Oxford: Oxford University Press.

Fish, S. (1982). Working on the chain gang: Interpretation in the law and in literary criticism. *Critical Inquiry*, 9(1): 201–216. https://doi.org/10.1086/448195.

Flanagan, B., & Hannikainen, I. R. (2022). The folk concept of law: Law is intrinsically moral. *Australasian Journal of Philosophy*, 100(1): 165–179. https://doi.org/10.1080/00048402.2020.1833953.

Foot, P. (2001). *Natural goodness*. Oxford: Oxford University Press.

Fuller, L. (1978). *The morality of law* (Rev. ed., 15. print). New Haven, CT: Yale University Press.

Gardner, J. (2001). Legal positivism: 51/2 myths. *The American Journal of Jurisprudence*, 46(1): 199–227. https://doi.org/10.1093/ajj/46.1.199.

Gardner, J. (2012). *Law as a leap of faith: Essays on law in general*. USA: Oxford University Press.

Geach, P. (1956). Good and evil. *Analysis*, 17: 33–42.

Gibbard, A. (2003). *Thinking how to live*. Cambridge: Harvard University Press.

Goodman, N., & Quine, W. V. (1947). Steps toward a constructive nominalism. *Journal of Symbolic Logic*, 12(4): 105–122. https://doi.org/10.2307/2266485.

Green, L., & Adams, T. (2019). Legal positivism. In E. N. Zalta (ed.), *The Stanford encyclopedia of philosophy.* https://plato.stanford.edu/archives/win2019/entries/legal-positivism/.

Greenberg, M. (2004). How facts make law. *Legal Theory*, 10(3): 157–198. https://doi.org/10.1017/S1352325204040212.

Greenberg, M. (2008). Hartian positivism and normative facts: How facts make law II. In S. Hershovitz (ed.), *Exploring law's empire*: The jurisprudence of Ronald Dworkin, 265–290.

Greenberg, M. (2014). The moral impact theory of law. *Yale Law Journal*, 123: 1288.

Grey, T. C. (1978). Origins of the unwritten constitution: Fundamental law in American revolutionary thought. *Stanford Law Review*, 30(5): 843.

Hamburger, P. A. (1993). Natural rights, natural law, and American constitutions. *Yale Law Journal*, 102(4): 907.

Hannikainen, I. R., Tobia, K. P., De Almeida, G. D. F. C. F., et al. (2021). Are there cross-cultural legal principles? Modal reasoning uncovers procedural constraints on law. *Cognitive Science*, 45(8), e13024.

Hart, H. L. A. (1958). Positivism and the separation of law and morals. *Harvard Law Review*, 71(4): 593. https://doi.org/10.2307/1338225.

Hart, H. L. A. (1994). *The concept of law* (2nd ed.). UK: Oxford University Press.

Hedden, B., & Nebel, J. M. (2024). Multidimensional Concepts and Disparate Scale Types. *Philosophical Review*, 133(3): 265–308 .

Helmholz, R. H. (2015). *Natural law in court: A history of legal theory in practice*. Cambridge: Harvard University Press.

Hershovitz, S. (2014). The end of jurisprudence. *Yale Law Journal*, 1234: 882–1345.

Hershovitz, S. (2023). *Law is a moral practice*. Cambridge: Harvard University Press.

Hilpinen, R. (1993). Authors and artifacts. *Proceedings of the Aristotelian Society*, 93: 155–178.

Hirsch, E. (2002). Against revisionary ontology. *Philosophical Topics*, 30(1): 103–127. https://doi.org/10.5840/philtopics20023013.

Horgan, T., & Timmons, M. (1991). New wave moral realism meets moral twin earth. *Journal of Philosophical Research*, 16: 447–465. https://doi.org/10.5840/jpr_1991_19.

Horwich, P. (2005). *Reflections on meaning* (1st ed.). Oxford: Oxford University Press. https://doi.org/10.1093/019925124X.001.0001.

Jackson, F. (1998). *From metaphysics to ethics: A defence of conceptual analysis*. UK: Oxford University Press.

Jiménez, F. (2023). Legal positivism for legal officials. *Canadian Journal of Law & Jurisprudence*, 36(2): 359–386. https://doi.org/10.1017/cjlj.2022.36.

Judy, T. (2008). *Normativity*. USA: Open Court Publishing.

Knobe, J., Prasada, S., & Newman, G. E. (2013). Dual character concepts and the normative dimension of conceptual representation. *Cognition*, 127(2): 242–257. https://doi.org/10.1016/j.cognition.2013.01.005.

Korman, D. Z. (2009). Eliminativism and the challenge from folk belief. *Noûs*, 43(2): 242–264. https://doi.org/10.1111/j.1468-0068.2009.00705.x.

Kovacs, D. M. (2018). The deflationary theory of ontological dependence. *The Philosophical Quarterly*, 68(272): 481–502. https://doi.org/10.1093/pq/pqy003.

Kovacs, D. M. (2019). How to be an uncompromising revisionary ontologist. *Synthese*, 198(3): 2129–2152. https://doi.org/10.1007/s11229-019-02196-8.

Kramer, M. H. (2004). *Where law and morality meet*. New York: Oxford University Press.

Kramer, M. H. (2007a). *Objectivity and the rule of law*. Cambridge: Cambridge University Press.

Kramer, M. H. (2007b). When is there not one right answer? *American Journal of Jurisprudence*, 53: 49–68.

Kramer, M. H. (2018). *H.L.A Hart*. Medford: Polity.

Kripke, S. (1980). *Naming and Necessity*. Cambridge: Harvard University Press.

Kripke, S. (1982). *Wittgenstein on rules and private language*. Cambridg: Harvard University Press.

Kubala, R. (2019). Literary Intentionalism. *Metaphilosophy*, 50(4): 503–515.

Kubala, R. (2021). Aesthetic practices and normativity. *Philosophy and Phenomenological Research*, 103(2): 408–425.

Leiter, B. (1995). Legal indeterminacy. *Legal Theory*, 1: 481–492.

Leiter, B. (2004). The end of empire: Dworkin and jurisprudence in the 21st century. *Rutgers Law Journal*, 36: 165–181.

Leiter, B. (2009). Explaining theoretical disagreement. *University of Chicago Law Review*, 76: 1215–1250. https://doi.org/10.2139/ssrn.1004768.

Leiter, B. (2011). The demarcation problem in jurisprudence: A new case for scepticism. *Oxford Journal of Legal Studies*, 31(4): 663–677.

Leiter, B. (2021). Legal positivism as a realist theory of law. In T. Spaak (ed.), *The Cambridge companion to legal positivism*. New York: Cambridge University Press, 79–102.

Levinson, J. (1980). What a musical work is. *The Journal of Philosophy*, 77(1): 5–28.

Lewis, D. (1975). Languages and language. In K. Gunderson (ed.), *Language, mind, and knowledge*. Minneapolis: University of Minnesota Press, 3–35.

Lewis, D. (1983). New work for a theory of universals. *Australasian Journal of Philosophy*, 61(4): 343–377. https://doi.org/10.1080/00048408312341131.

Lewis, D. (1984). Putnam's Paradox. *Australasian Journal of Philosophy*, 62(3): 221–236. https://doi.org/10.1080/00048408412340013.

Liao, S., Meskin, A., & Knobe, J. (2020). Dual character art concepts. *Pacific Philosophical Quarterly*, 101(1): 102–128. https://doi.org/10.1111/papq.12301.

Lindeman, K. (2017). Constitutivism without normative thresholds. *Journal of Ethics and Social Philosophy*, 12(3): 231–258. https://doi.org/10.26556/jesp.v12i3.220.

Mackie, J. L. (1977). *Ethics: inventing right and wrong*. New York: Penguin Books.

Mag Uidhir, C. (2013). *Art and art-attempts*. Oxford: Oxford University Press.

Mag Uidhir, C., & Magnus, P. D. (2011). Art concept pluralism. *Metaphilosophy*, 42(1–2): 83–97.

Marmor, A. (2004a). The rule of law & its limits. *Law & Philosophy*, 23: 1.

Marmor, A. (2004b). Exclusive legal positivism. In J. Coleman, K. Himma, & S. Shapiro (eds.), *The Oxford handbook of jurisprudence and philosophy of law*. New York: Oxford University Press, 104–124.

Marmor, A. (2005). *Interpretation and legal theory* (2nd ed.). USA: Hart.

Marmor, A. (2007). The ideal of the rule of law. In D. Patterson (ed.), *A companion to philosophy of law and legal theory*. Hoboken: Blackwell Publishing, 666–674.

Marmor, A. (2011). *Philosophy of law*. Princeton: Princeton University Press.

Marmor, A. (2013). Farewell to conceptual analysis (in jurisprudence). In W. J. Waluchow, & S. Sciaraffa (eds.), *Philosophical foundations of the nature of law*. Oxford: Oxford University Press, 209–229.

McGrath, S. (2014). Relax? Don't do it! Why moral realism won't come cheap. *Oxford Studies in Metaethics*, 9: 186–214.

McPherson, T., & Plunkett, D. (2024). Metaethics and the conceptual ethics of normativity. *Inquiry*, 67(1): 93–126. https://doi.org/10.1080/0020174X.2021.1873177.

Millikan, R. G. (1984). *Language, thought, and other biological categories*. USA: The MIT Press.

Moore, M. (1992). Law as a functional kind. In R. George (ed.), *Natural law theory: Contemporary essays*. Oxford: Oxford University Press.

Murphy, L. (2001). The political question of the concept of law. In J. Coleman (ed.), *Hart's postscript: Essays on the postscript to "the concept of law."* New York: Oxford University Press, 371–409.

Murphy, M. C. (2001). *Natural law and practical rationality.* Cambridge: Cambridge University Press.

Murphy, M. C. (2005). Natural law theory. In M. P. Golding & W. A. Edmundson (eds.), *The Blackwell guide to the philosophy of law & legal theory.* UK: Wiley-Blackwell.

Murphy, M. C. (2006). *Natural law in jurisprudence and politics.* Cambridge: Cambridge University Press.

Murphy, M. C. (2012). Defect and deviance in natural law jurisprudence. In M. Klatt (ed.), *Institutionalized reason: The jurisprudence of Robert Alexy.* Oxford: Oxford University Press, 45–60.

Neta, R. (2004). On the normative significance of brute facts. *Legal Theory,* 10(3): 199–214. https://doi.org/10.1017/S1352325204040224.

Nye, H. (2021). The one-system view and Dworkin's anti-archimedean eliminativism. *Law and Philosophy,* 40: 247–276.

Peacocke, C. (1992). *A study of concepts.* Cambridge: MIT Press.

Pettit, P. (2023). *The State.* Princeton: Princeton University Press.

Plunkett, D. (2012). A positivist route for explaining how facts make law. *Legal Theory,* 18(2): 139–207. https://doi.org/10.1017/S1352325212000079.

Plunkett, D. (2013). Legal positivism and the moral aim thesis. *Oxford Journal of Legal Studies,* 33(3): 563–605.

Plunkett, D. (2016). Negotiating the meaning of "law": The metalinguistic dimension of the dispute over legal positivism. *Legal Theory,* 22(3–4): 205–275. https://doi.org/10.1017/S1352325216000070.

Plunkett, D., & Phillips, J. (2023). Are there really any dual-character concepts? *Philosophical Perspectives,* 37(1): 340–369.

Plunkett, D., & Sundell, T. (2013a). Disagreement and the semantics of normative and evaluative terms. *Philosophers' Imprint,* 13(23): 1–37.

Plunkett, D., & Sundell, T. (2013b). Dworkin's interpretivism and the pragmatics of legal disputes. *Legal Theory,* 19(3): 242–281.

Pollock, F. (1902). The history of the law of nature: A preliminary study. *Columbia Law Review,* 2(3): 131.

Postema, G. J. (2018). Time in law's domain. *Ratio Juris,* 31(2): 160–182.

Postema, G. J. (2019). *Bentham and the common law tradition* (2nd ed.). Oxford: Oxford University Press.

Price, P. J. (1997). Natural law and birthright citizenship in Calvin's case (1608). *Yale Journal Law & Humanities,* 9: 73–145.

Priel, D. (2020). Analytic jurisprudence in time. In T. Bustamante, & T. Decat (eds.), *Philosophy of law as an integral part of philosophy: Essays on the jurisprudence of Gerald J. Postema*. New York: Hart, 213–241.

Putnam, H. (1973). Meaning and reference. *The Journal of Philosophy*, 70(19): 699. https://doi.org/10.2307/2025079.

Rabin, G. O. (2020). Toward a theory of concept mastery: The recognition view. *Erkenntnis*, 85: 627–648.

Radbruch, G. (1973). Gesetzliches Unrecht und ubergesetzliches Recht. In E. Wolf, & H. P. Schneider (eds.), *Rechtsphilosophie* (8th ed.). Stuttgart: K. F. Koehler.

Railton, P. (2019). We'll see you in court! The rule of law as an explanatory and normative kind. In D. Plunkett et al. (ed.), *New essays on metaethics and jurisprudence*. USA: Oxford University Press, 1–22.

Raz, J. (1979). *The authority of law*. New York: Oxford University Press.

Raz, J. (1985). Authority, law and morality. *The Monist*, 68: 295–324.

Raz, J. (1994). *Ethics in the public domain: Essays in the morality of law and politics*. Oxford: Clarendon Press.

Raz, J. (1999). *Practical reasons and norms*. Oxford: Oxford University Press.

Raz, J. (2004). Can there be a theory of law. In M. Golding, & W. Edmundson (eds.), *Blackwell guide to philosophy of law and legal theory*. UK: Blackwell, 324–342.

Raz, J. (2019). The law's own virtue. *Oxford Journal of Legal Studies*, 39: 1–15.

Raz, J. (2002). *Practical reasons and norms*. Oxford: Oxford University Press.

Rosen, G. (2010). Metaphysical dependence: Grounding and reduction. In B. Hale, & A. Hoffman (eds.), *Modality: Metaphysics, logics, and epistemology*, 109–136. Oxford: Oxford University Press.

Rudolph, R. E. (2023). Contested metalinguistic negotiation. *Synthese*, 202: 90.

Ryu, A. (2024). How reasons make law. *Oxford Journal of Legal Studies*, 24: 133.

Salinger, E. (2023). Expressivism and moral independence. *Philosophy and Phenomenological Research*, 108(1): 136–152.

Scanlon, T. (forthcoming, 2025). Understanding good of a kind and good for in terms of reasons. In K. Brownlee, D. Enoch, & A. Marmor (eds.), *Engaging Raz*. Oxford University Press.

Schroeter, L. (2012). Bootstrapping our way to samesaying. *Synthese*, 189: 177–197.

Shapiro, S. J. (2007). The "Hart-Dworkin" debate: A short guide for the perplexed. In A. Ripstein (ed.), *Ronald Dworkin*. Cambridge: Cambridge University Press, 22–49.

Shapiro, S. J. (2011). *Legality*. Cambridge: Harvard University Press.

Simmonds, N. (2008). *Law as a moral idea*. Oxford: Oxford University Press.
Smith, D. (2015). Agreement and disagreement in law. *Canadian Journal of Law & Jurisprudence*, 28: 183.
Smith, M. (2013). A constitutivist theory of reasons: Its promise and parts. *Law, Ethics, and Philosophy*, 1: 9–30.
Smithson, R. (2020). Metaphysical and conceptual grounding. *Erkenntnis*, 85(6): 1501–1525. https://doi.org/10.1007/s10670-018-0088-3.
Solum, L. B. (2015). The fixation thesis: The role of historical fact in original meaning. *Notre Dame Law Review*, 91: 1.
Soper, P. (1986). Choosing a legal theory on moral grounds. *Social Philosophy and Policy*, 4(1): 31–48. https://doi.org/10.1017/S026505250000042X.
Soper, P. (2007). In defense of classical natural law in legal theory: Why unjust law is no law at all. *Canadian Journal of Law & Jurisprudence*, 20(1): 201–223. https://doi.org/10.1017/S0841820900005750.
Sunstein, C. R. (1996). *Legal reasoning and political conflict*. Oxford: Oxford University Press.
Thomasson, A. (2007). *Ordinary objects*. Oxford: Oxford University Press.
Thomasson, A. L. (2003). Realism and human kinds. *Philosophy and Phenomenological Research*, 67(3): 580–609. https://doi.org/10.1111/j.1933-1592.2003.tb00309.x.
Thomson, J. J. (2008). *Normativity*. Chicago: Open Court.
Tobia, K. (2022). Experimental jurisprudence. *The University of Chicago Law Review*, 89(3): 735–802.
Toh, K. (2005). Hart's expressivism and his benthamite project. *Legal Theory*, 11(2): 75–123.
Toh, K. (2011). Legal judgments as plural acceptance of norms. In L. Green, & B. Leiter (eds.), *Oxford studies in philosophy of law: Volume 1*. Oxford: Oxford University Press, 107–137.
Tripkovic, B., & Patterson, D. (2023). The promise and limits of grounding in law. *Legal Theory*, 29(3): 202–228. https://doi.org/10.1017/S1352325223000149.
Valentini, L. (2024). *Morality and socially constructed norms*. Oxford: Oxford University Press.
van Roojen, M. (2023). Moral cognitivism vs. non-cognitivism. In E. N. Zalta, & U. Nodelman (eds.), *The Stanford encyclopedia of philosophy* (Winter 2023 ed.). https://plato.stanford.edu/archives/win2023/entries/moral-cognitivism/.
Vander Waerdt, P. A. (1994). Philosophical influence on Roman jurisprudence? The case of stoicism and natural law. In *Aufstieg und Niedergang der römischen Welt (ANRW)/Rise and decline of the Roman world*. Berlin: De Gruyter, 4851–4901.

Waldron, J. (2001). Normative (or ethical) positivism. In J. L. Coleman (ed.), *Hart's postscript: Essays on the postscript to "the concept of law."* New York: Oxford University Press, 410–433.

Waldron, J. (2008). Positivism and legality: Hart's equivocal response to Fuller. *NYU Law Review*, 83(4): 1135–1169.

Waldron, J. (2008b). The concept and the rule of law. *Georgia Law Review*, 43: 1–61.

Waluchow, W. (1994). *Inclusive legal positivism.* Oxford: Oxford University Press.

Watson, B. (2022a). In defense of the standard picture: What the standard picture explains that the moral impact theory cannot. *Legal Theory*, 28(1): 59–88. https://doi.org/10.1017/S1352325221000276.

Watson, B. (2022b). The decline of natural law and the rise of exclusive positivism. *SMU Law Review Forum*, 75(1): 174–190. https://doi.org/10.25172/slrf.75.1.4.

Watson, B. (2023). How to answer Dworkin's argument from theoretical disagreement without attributing confusion or disingenuity to legal officials. *Canadian Journal of Law & Jurisprudence*, 36(1): 215–240.

Wright, L. (1973). Functions. *The Philosophical Review*, 82: 139–168.

Yale, D. E. C. (1974). Iudex in propria causa: An historical excursus. *Cambridge Law Journal*, 33: 80–96.

Zalta, E. (2006). Essence and modality. *Mind*, 115: 659–693.

Acknowledgments

I am grateful to audiences at Columbia University, Cambridge University, Oxford University, Yale University, and the Philadelphia Normative Philosophy Conference for their questions and comments on presentations based on the second and third sections. I received especially helpful feedback from Rachel Schutz, Bill Watson, Andrei Marmor, Crescente Molina, Amin Afrouzi, Matthew Kramer, David Enoch, Xi Zhang, Samantha Godwin, Shelly Kagan, Brian Leiter, Angelo Ryu, and two anonymous reviewers. The editors of the Cambridge Elements Series in the Philosophy of Law – Kenneth Ehrenberg, George Pavlakos, and Gerald Postema – are owed a special thanks for their invitation to contribute to the series. This volume has helped me synthesize my work in legal philosophy over the last five years. The views I defend in Sections 2.4 and 3.3 build on observations in Atiq (2019, 2020a), Section 2.1 offers an abridged version of the argument in Atiq (2023), and Section 2.5 summarizes and further develops an argument in Atiq (forthcoming).

Cambridge Elements

Philosophy of Law

Series Editors
George Pavlakos
University of Glasgow

George Pavlakos is Professor of Law and Philosophy at the School of Law, University of Glasgow. He has held visiting posts at the universities of Kiel and Luzern, the European University Institute, the UCLA Law School, the Cornell Law School and the Beihang Law School in Beijing. He is the author of *Our Knowledge of the Law* (2007) and more recently has co-edited *Agency, Negligence and Responsibility* (2021) and *Reasons and Intentions in Law and Practical Agency* (2015).

Gerald J. Postema
University of North Carolina at Chapel Hill

Gerald J. Postema is Professor Emeritus of Philosophy at the University of North Carolina at Chapel Hill. Among his publications count *Utility, Publicity, and Law: Bentham's Moral and Legal Philosophy* (2019); *On the Law of Nature, Reason, and the Common Law: Selected Jurisprudential Writings of Sir Matthew Hale* (2017); *Legal Philosophy in the Twentieth Century: The Common Law World* (2011), *Bentham and the Common Law Tradition*, 2nd edition (2019).

Kenneth M. Ehrenberg
University of Surrey

Kenneth M. Ehrenberg is Professor of Jurisprudence and Philosophy at the University of Surrey School of Law and Co-Director of the Surrey Centre for Law and Philosophy. He is the author of *The Functions of Law* (2016) and numerous articles on the nature of law, jurisprudential methodology, the relation of law to morality, practical authority, and the epistemology of evidence law.

Associate Editor
Sally Zhu
University of Sheffield

Sally Zhu is a Lecturer in Property Law at University of Sheffield. Her research is on property and private law aspects of platform and digital economies.

About the Series

This series provides an accessible overview of the philosophy of law, drawing on its varied intellectual traditions in order to showcase the interdisciplinary dimensions of jurisprudential enquiry, review the state of the art in the field, and suggest fresh research agendas for the future. Focussing on issues rather than traditions or authors, each contribution seeks to deepen our understanding of the foundations of the law, ultimately with a view to offering practical insights into some of the major challenges of our age.

Cambridge Elements

Philosophy of Law

Elements in the Series

Revisiting the Rule of Law
Kristen Rundle

The Place of Coercion in Law
Triantafyllos Gkouvas

The Differentiation and Autonomy of Law
Emilios Christodoulidis

The Moral Prerequisites of the Criminal Law: Legal Moralism and the Problem of Mala Prohibita
Ambrose Y. K. Lee and Alexander F. Sarch

Legal Personhood
Visa A. J. Kurki

The Philosophy of Legal Proof
Lewis Ross

Content-Independence in Law: Possibility and Potential
Julie Dickson

The Normativity of Law
Michael Giudice

Legal Rights and Moral Rights
Matthew H. Kramer

Dignity and Rights
Ariel Zylberman

Subsidiarity
Andreas Follesdal

Contemporary Non-Positivism
Emad H. Atiq

A full series listing is available at: www.cambridge.org/EPHL

For EU product safety concerns, contact us at Calle de José Abascal, 56–1°, 28003 Madrid, Spain or eugpsr@cambridge.org.

www.ingramcontent.com/pod-product-compliance
Ingram Content Group UK Ltd.
Pitfield, Milton Keynes, MK11 3LW, UK
UKHW030645250425
457871UK00018B/267